Saul you're destined for great things to make the world a better place.

BREAKTHROUGH THINKING

ೞ೩೦

From Mediocre to Extraordinary
~ Living from the Mind of Christ

By Dr Gershom Sikaala

BREAKTHROUGH THINKING
BY DR GERSHOM SIKAALA

Published by Gershom Sikaala

ISBN 978-1-61422-792-2

Published March 2018 (334 pages)

Compilation and Typesetting: Adele Visser of AVCA
e-mail: visser969@gmail.com | www.visser969.wix.com/avca

Cover: Adam Engela of 7Genesis
e-mail: adam@7genesis.co.za | www.7genesis.co.za

Editor: Catherine Jansen

Printed in United States of America.

Founder of Hollywood Mastery Class in California;
Zambikes International Business; His Presence Fire Ministries;
United Nations Inter-faith Goodwill Ambassador;
Awarded National Statesman

www.gershomsikaala.org
gershomsikaala@yahoo.com

This book is lovingly dedicated to
the Lord Jesus Christ
who gave us full restoration of His mind.

ENDORSEMENTS

"Dr. Sikaala's message is full of hope, faith and the supernatural assurance that all eternal fruit in our lives come from intimacy with Jesus. I pray his words would strengthen and encourage you to live a life wholly devoted to our Father in heaven. Every day I am thankful to seek the King side by side with such passionate believers. Dr. Sikaala's life and mission is a true blessing to the Lord's wonderful, ever-growing church ~ in Zambia, in Africa, and all around the world."

Heidi G. Baker.
PhD Co-founder and President of Iris Global

"Breakthrough Thinking, by Dr. Gershom Sikaala, will go down in Christian history as one of the most important books ever written on breaking all limitations to human potential through activating, throughout mankind, the "Christ Mind!" Without any argument, there is no mind loftier than the Mind of Christ. This book follows the order of Christian classics like Oswald Chamber's "My Highest for His Utmost!" You will receive a real and life-changing breakthrough when you receive the revelation contained within these anointed pages."

Dr. Francis Myles Senior Pastor, Royal Priesthood Int. Embassy, Tempe, AZ. Bestselling author of "The Order of Melchizedek"

"Breakthrough Thinking" is a masterpiece of revelation, insight and wisdom. It is a valuable, indepth study that is both eminently practical and readily applicable to our daily life and the human

condition. Dr. Gershom Sikaala is a brilliant thinker, strategic leader, successful entrepreneur, ardent worshiper, glory carrier, healing evangelist and articulate communicator. This book is a must read for those who are serious and intentional about having and/or knowing the mind of Christ. To acquire the mind of Jesus is a costly, time consuming process and investment ~ which requires study, practice, discipline, sacrifice, obedience, maturity, dying to self; and saying "No" to other, lesser minds which are counterfeits and poor substitutes for the authentic, original, real thing and genuine article. But it is well worth the effort and will pay rich dividends and eternal rewards. Not having the mind of Christ is not a Scriptural option for believers, as we are commanded to "have this same mind in you." Therefore, this book will help many people. Buy it, read it, live it, share it!

Dr. Bruce Cook
Kingdom Congressional International Alliance

"Breakthrough Thinking by Prophet Gershom Sikaala has my stamp of approval. I know that the Devil cannot influence your mind if your mind is stayed on God. There are always qualifications for the promises God gives us in His word. To remain in this perfectly, we have to fix our eyes on Jesus. The pollution in the minds of people is keeping them from having a single vision. Breakthrough Thinking requires a deliberate focus on God and His promises. Gershom has done the Body of Christ a great service in writing this powerful book."

Paul Cain Ministries International
Santa Maria, CA

5

"Dr. Gershom Sikaala has written a book that has a modern-day global voice for the Spirit of God. His writings will show you how to access the heavenly mind and bring it to earth in a divine mindset. He truly is masterful at explaining the heart and mind of God for His creation. This is a global message for our generation today, and I highly recommend the reading of Dr. Sikaala's timely revelations in this book."

Dr. Clyde Rivers
Golden Rule World Peace Ambassador Founder, President:
IChange Nations

"I have personally experienced the grace of God on Gershom Sikaala pertaining revival, the glory of God and his heart to reach California and America. Gershom is a large part of the "stadium" movement and for many years has left his mark on church revival around the world. Gershom's heart is for souls and "Breakthrough Thinking" is an overview of the present movement to further the blessing and inheritance afforded to all believers through our Lord Jesus Christ and what He secured for us through the cross and the resurrection. Our God created us in His richness and in perfect love. And He loves every soul with A Perfect God-kind of Love and desires that not one should perish. The same God has created us in the fashion of abundant inheritance and fullness of blessings to affect the world around us. Thank you Gershom for this labor of Love and enrichment!"

David Andrade
Line In the Sand International

"As you read the powerful pages of Dr. Gershom Sikaala's book, Breakthrough Thinking, your life will soar to new realms of victorious living. God's Word will wash out the limiting negative thoughts of the past, replacing them with the unlimiting thoughts of Christ. You will discover the joy and victory of living, and thinking with a 'renewed mind' ~ the very mind of Christ Himself, where all things are possible."

Dr. A.L. Gill
A.L Gill's Ministries International

"Breakthrough Thinking is about seeing the future as it should be. When we get to heaven we are going to experience a supernatural impartation of God's mind. Can you imagine the power of that? Prophet Gershom Sikaala's book on "Breakthrough Thinking" is like receiving an impartation of the Mind of God... before you get to heaven. I know that one of the end-time strategies of the devil is to capture the "MIND", especially the minds of millennials. In "Breakthrough Thinking" Gershom creates a roadmap for stopping the enemy from stealing and abusing your mind. You can become a "Breakthrough Thinker" today, because you have access to the mind of Christ. I highly recommend this book to all seekers of truth."

Dr. Ralph Wilkerson
Founder of Melodyland Christian Center - Anaheim, CA

PREFACE

The content of this book is aimed to blow your mind! First of all, to clean out the old cobwebs, and to present to you how to activate what you already have in Christ. The restoration of humankind is available to all who believe in Jesus Christ. He desires every human being to be whole in spirit, soul and body.

The rebirth of our spirits enables the possibility of receiving the mind of Christ. Christianity has, however, not been effective enough regarding the positive manifestation of this in the natural realm. My prayer through this writing is to create an awareness of the great treasury of heavenly thinking, and to extend an eternal invitation to return to the original way God intended you to operate!

My intention is not to be intellectual or scientific or even to convey an opinion, but to spark an experiential knowledge of the depths of the infinite mind of the Creator. As always, referencing is from personal revelations from the Bible by the Holy Spirit. I especially used the Amplified translation as it provides a broader ability to quote within context.

I am more than confident that receiving the mind of Christ by faith can reach and impact you right where you are, without prejudice. From the greatest to the simplest minds qualify for this divine gift ~ from greatest theologians of all denominations, brilliant philosophers, and students to the ordinary man on the street.

Thinking like Christ means you are inseparably connected to heaven's faith realm to operate optimally in spirit, soul and body. In this tri-part synergy, your renewed perspective carries the wealth of a heart-change and a desire to become one with Jesus as He prayed in the garden (John 17). And in so doing, becoming *like* Him in thought, speech and action.

If you need courage to advance in faith, this writing is for you! God intended us not to only grow but to shine with His glory! His Word is our treasure from which we delve ~ a renewed mind to bring about the living reality of walking in the glory realm of the covenant lifestyle.

With this in mind, one of the main aims of this book is to bring a renewed perspective about wealth. Regarding spiritual wealth, Christianity has never failed, as long as believers are genuinely connected to Jesus. But somehow, we have limited understanding of His *heart* ~ specifically about His purpose for wealth, health and success. Our greatest need in these times is a true and greater connection with the Lord, which will manifest His divine generous nature to be modeled to a crumbling world.

I agree in prayer with you today for the opening of eyes and ears as you read about the heartbeat of the Lord for your life (Eph. 1:18).

Sketching a quick overview of spiritual restoration discussed, I touch on not only intellectual wealth, but also that of spirit and body (health and finance).

Regarding **intellectual** wealth, we will discuss varied Scriptural evidence highlighting God's overflow, resources and abundance reserved for the hungry and thirsty righteous. Radical believers have the solution to the world. They simply and bravely receive the mind of Christ, and demonstrate the lifestyle of this wisdom ~ they have the intellectual capacity of God. Like Jesus said, *"Verily, verily"*, I want to say, verily, a greater movement of an abundance of wealthy Christian minds, operating with purified, open hearts affecting each sphere of society ~ is available to all who believe and receive it from the Lord.

Regarding health and financial wealth ~ the body of Christ must receive their rightful **inheritance**. We were created to not only display the glory of God from a place of His gifting, but to also combat lack and bring true, heavenly wealth and riches to earth; and to consider the importance of fulfilling proper "religious acts" (James 1:27) according to God's standards ~ caring for the poor, widows and orphans, and to also keep ourselves uncontaminated by the world.

Bringing physical change to an environment is evidence of restoration in the spirit of our minds; and therefore an advancement to the "greater works" of John 14:12 ~ things greater than those recorded in the Gospels and the book of Acts. Let your vision be lifted higher to that which God has prepared for you personally today ~ beyond what you can think, dream or imagine!

Do you know that you are the **fulfillment** of Scripture that the glory of Jesus will be seen in the nations? Will you accept the invitation to be the glorious Bride who carries spiritual and economic solutions to the hopeless?

The **relevance** of this book, released in the year 2016, is so that through the illumination of the mind of Christ, an impenetrable barrier to the fear and terror attacking our planet is offered. Our grasp of the Messiah, the Savior, will prevent any gates of hell to prevail against us in these end times.

When heavenly thinking becomes the **lifestyle** of the majority of Christians, God's voice and principles will be released to the nations. And, as our callings grow, we will also grow in **financial** wealth! Even those searching for the true voice will find truth and reality not just in our preaching, teaching and discipleship. They will witness **fruitfulness** in our faith in Jesus being manifest through our testimony of His glorious restoration and generosity affecting our spirit, soul and body.

This is certainly a provocative book, a challenge to Christians to fundamentally believe God for His undeniable will to prosper us. Prosperity will no longer be a controversial topic as it has been over the years. The strategy of the enemy will come into

the light – the taint of the incomplete truth will only be an education to us to not repeat the cycle of slavery.

The end-time church will have resolution to really search deeply into the **absolute truth** of the mind of Christ ~ since the success of our exploits depends upon this vital revelation.

ೞ

ෲ

Ephesians 3:20 (Amp)

"Now to Him who is able to [carry out His purpose and] do superabundantly more than all that we dare ask or think [infinitely beyond our greatest prayers, hopes, or dreams], according to His power that is at work within us"

ෲ

CONTENTS

PART 1
THE HEAVENLY MIND

CHAPTER 1
ETERNALLY MINDED

ROMANS 11:33-36 (AMP)

"Oh, the depth of the riches and wisdom and knowledge of God! How unsearchable are His judgments and decisions and how unfathomable and untraceable are His ways! For who has known the mind of the Lord, or who has been His counselor? Or who has first given to Him that it would be paid back to Him? For from Him [all things originate] and through Him [all things live and exist] and to Him are all things [directed]. To Him be glory and honor forever! Amen."

MORE than understanding how the human mind works, each person has a vital and basic need to know their eternal Creator. My prayer is that this book will not only bring a change of mind through Christ, but more importantly about a change of heart which begins with *knowing* God Himself and so becoming eternally minded.

Even though it is an impossibility to understand the scope of the mind of God, the indwelling Holy Spirit provides extraordinary and supernatural *access* to the mind of Christ in order to know His ways, His truth and His life. As we walk by faith, each dependent step will reveal His light.

COVENANT CONNECTION

John 14:6 (NKJ)

"Jesus said to him [Thomas], I am the way, the truth, and the life. No one comes to the Father except through Me."

This privilege of access is not attained ~ it is inherited through accepting a covenant with God through Christ.

As a boy growing up in Zambia, I was not privileged to have access to the comforts and opportunities of first-world living, yet my heart connecting with God brought me into full proximity of all the royal and empowering benefits of the heavenlies. Likewise, a prince or princess born in a royal line has not attained wealth, privilege and honor through works, but by birth.

Before you continue reading, take an uninterrupted moment to freely give your heart and life to the Lord Jesus Christ. With this right to become a child of God (John 1:12-13), you are enabled to clothe your body and mind in His provision for you. I invite you, while reading this book, to not only input information into your mind, but to better know the *person* of Jesus Christ in your heart.

Through the transformation of the heart, the mind is brought into renewal. In the process you are becoming eternally minded through the guidance of the Holy Spirit. He brings you to the reality of being eternally conscious, just like God revealed Himself to Moses as "I am" in the burning bush. Observe for a few moments the statement Jesus extends to you: *"I am the way, the truth, and the life. No one comes to the Father except through Me"* (John 14:6).

The only true way for your life is by the light He provides, and the truth that is the foundation on which you build. His breath is the very source from which you will produce an extraordinary mind ~ and thereby a supernatural, abundant life.

SYNERGY OF LIGHT

John 1:3-5 (NKJ)

"All things were made through Him, and without Him nothing was made that was made. In Him was life and the life was the light of men. And the light shines in the darkness, and the darkness did not comprehend it"

Now that you are eternally and vitally connected, you have synergy with heaven and with your eternal purpose on earth. You have the source of light streaming through your spirit, mind and body! Let that sink in for a few moments.

Let us now venture further a little on a few thoughts of our origin and the importance of our connection with the mind of Christ, our source of life.

Most people have a built-in desire to explore and enjoy nature, and especially, knowing more about the universe. In the process they discover more about themselves. As the sun spectacularly provides light to an entire solar system, so God provides complete illumination to our world. As He is the eternal center of our existence, He is also the everlasting source from which we originate.

Therefore, being connected with God is truly becoming eternally alive! Staying connected with Him is living abundantly.

God created us for connection ~ physically *and* spiritually. Within this synergy, we are not just breathing or surviving, we are plugged into His glory ~ not only temporally but eternally.

This eternal light being switched on by mere acceptance of it has from the beginning become an agent of divine dominion. This light brings creative, vibrant, ongoing change and development in our spiritual and physical environments.

Allow your mind to be saturated with this principle from Genesis, by which God creates order and dominion. He uses the power of His light-filled words to create light. You are a like Him, a "light being" creating life from the source within!

Genesis 1:2-3 (NKJ)

"The earth was without form, and void; and darkness was on the face of the deep. And the Spirit of God was hovering over the face of the waters. Then God said, "Let there be light"; and there was light"

21

From this truth, see your heart and mind as a beacon of light for everything created (including how your mind works) originating from the realm of light ~ the eternal Spirit realm.

As recorded in Genesis, from the source of this unending, pure spiritual light, God created a host of physical celestial bodies.

After six days of spectacular work, I imagine He, like an artist, took a day off to step back from His work to inspect and approve it. He declared all of it as "*good*" (Gen. 1:6-25). He is still declaring this over your life today, so you need to grasp the attitude and mindset that you *are* very good!

The same commission God gave to Adam at the beginning of time is what He is still declaring over you. He is not only needing you to **"be fruitful and multiply, fill the earth and subdue it, have dominion"** (Gen. 1:28), but He commissioned you to be an extension of His eternal person of light. God originally created everything to last an eternity, since everything had the essence of His light in it. The light in you is immortal. Even though your body will age and grow weak, your spirit man is growing stronger by the day.

2 Corinthians 3:18 (Amp)

"And we all, with unveiled face, continually seeing as in a mirror the glory of the Lord are progressively being transformed into His image from [one degree of] glory to [even more] glory, which comes from the Lord, [who is] the Spirit"

I love to take walks on the beach or neighborhood to talk out loud with God. My most memorable times have been either times of sunrise or sunset, and I think of how it must've been like for Adam to meet with God *"in the cool of the day"* (Gen. 3:8). The next time you take a walk in either rising or fading light, think of how important our sun is to your everyday life.

Then imagine how, just like the sun, God illuminates the earth. Everything is brought to life by His glorious "blessing-rays". Now think how dependent you are on the nourishment provided through the heart and mind of Christ.

Think too, how easily your light can fade. The ancients had a partial understanding of the importance of light, but in their search for the true Creator, they focused on the creation. Studies show the extent of how these lost generations built their entire existence around the sun, moon and animals, which became their objects of worship and their concept of eternity. Just as this consequently led to their demise, a historic warning holds true of how quickly our own minds, thoughts and ways can radically eclipse and alter the source and meaning of true life. This can happen by focusing on the temporal and the seen, and not on the eternal light.

My life is an eternal testimony that a radical connection with God can light up a man who could have been consumed by darkness. Without Jesus, I would've been an abandoned, rejected and worthless person, not amounting to much.

His life shone on mine and suddenly my heart started coming alive and my mind started seeing my tremendous worth demonstrated through God sending Jesus to open heaven to me. His heavenly rays brought me focus and a purpose, and that is why I treasure Him above all else in this life.

My question to anybody finding themselves in a dark space or time in life is: What do you value the most? What and where is the light of your life? For what you spend most of your time with, is what you will end up valuing most. I invite you into the synergy of light in Jesus Christ, where your eyes will adjust to focusing on the invaluable and eternal things that bring life and joy. Reconnect again with the center of all things and you will notice how your increased perspective of self-value will grow and bring you into spiritual maturity as a son or daughter of God.

The Father desires to center your life by starting with your heart and mind. As you surrender and trust Him, He brings you to this very secure and peaceful place ~ a glorious way of thinking about Him and about yourself. As you meditate and act on the desire to discover the treasures of His Word and promises, you will realize that there's nothing more valuable than His presence and His thoughts working in you. You will find unnecessary, inappropriate and unfocused thinking becoming less and less active in your life.

You will realize that He is truly the only source of light and life in daily living.

I see our glorious, radiant Jesus beckoning you onto the road of light to walk with Him. He confidently says, *"I am the way"* (John 14:6). He knows you need His illuminated, resurrected presence to know which road to take.

As He is the originator of life, He will hold and keep you as you walk with Him ~ not only in the "cool of the day," but you will walk each day in the fullest, warmest glow of His love light.

Hebrews 1:3 (Amp)

"The Son is the radiance and only expression of the glory of [our awesome] God [reflecting God's Shekinah glory, the Light-being, the brilliant light of the divine],

and the exact representation and perfect imprint of His [Father's] essence, and upholding and maintaining and propelling all things [the entire physical and spiritual universe] by His powerful word [carrying the universe along to its predetermined goal]"

LIGHT FOR SIGHT

A South-African Christian businessman. was recently traveling to North Africa on business, when he met up with one of his associates conducting a business transaction over a few days. During their many hours waiting for the transaction to conclude in the hotel, they spoke about matters concerning their health.

The associate was complaining of having great back pain, when he confidently testified of his faith and how he had personally experienced divine healing. After enquiring to pray for the man, the power of God touched his back! But more importantly, he was more open for the Gospel to transform his life.

When the believer asked if the associate owned a Bible, he told of how another Christian had gifted him with one and how he had been drawn to read it, even though he had been raised Buddhist. Since then, his seeking heart grew more for the God of the Bible. He also developed a desire for Him to be personally involved in his life. He told of how, when he was reading the Bible, his heart was at peace but the words were obscure. The believer explained to him that the Bible is a spiritual book, and that it is a connection point for a relationship with the Lord. He then led the man to receive the Holy Spirit, for He is the "Helper" towards understanding the Bible (John 14:16). As soon as the man received the Spirit and asked Him to help him understand the Bible, his mind opened. He received light for sight!

From a quest to genuinely know the Lord of the Bible, a simple relational process starts taking place. Our hearts and ears are opened to really understand Him! Once we behold Him, we are also able to see ourselves truthfully from His perspective.

As you intentionally spend time with God, He gives life-gifts back to you ~ one of which is the gift of perfect thoughts! You will have the ideal heart approach, with astounding answers for every problem as you apply your Holy Spirit-driven listening skills in your commitment of partnering with Him.

Be aware that the world, or realm, of darkness cannot comprehend what you are producing in God because the Light blinds them. They will always be in the dark about the Holy Spirit, His gifts, why you are always smiling, and how you have such wisdom and solutions in life. Your connection with God will undoubtedly spark curiosity among unbelievers, so be prepared *"in season and out"* (2 Tim. 4:2) to give an account of your faith at any time.

THE LIGHT OF LIFE

Our original source of light, Jesus, said He is *"the life"* (John 14:6). The first creature that was formed from this source of life was Adam. He was also the only created being that personally received the breath, or Spirit, of God from His mouth. The breath of God in the Hebrew language is *"neshamah,"* a verb that means Adam was uniquely "taught to breathe". Animals also have a respiratory system, but they were not given the privileged and intimate lesson of the breath of God. We therefore should understand that above all in creation, we are a synergized product of His image, life and breath.

Genesis 1:26 (NKJ)

"Then God said, "Let Us make man in Our image, according to Our likeness, let them have dominion..."

Genesis 2:7 (NKJ)

"And the Lord God formed man of the dust of the ground, and breathed life into his nostrils the breath of life, and man became a living being"

In addition, our breath in God is the source of spiritual, physical and material wealth ~ including the wisdom and knowledge of God as an eternal treasury of both heart and mind. As our motive increasingly becomes focused not on the *gift* or treasury, but on the *Giver*, a transformation and renewal by association takes place. This inner light breath restores us to our original, eternal and glorious form. It is so deep; the depths are inexhaustible, for the understanding of Him is ever expanding.

The only guarantee, upon reaching a full understanding of the mind of Christ, is that it will last an eternity! It is therefore of utmost necessity, that each person not only attain the light of life, but also to live to comprehend the *eternal* meaning of life ~ to know God and embrace the gift of eternal life. This gift is not to only hold, or receive life, but to enable us to become a giver of life. Our eternal Savior and Champion of life, Jesus Christ, modeled this. A simple choice is therefore set before each individual ~ to either walk in His light, or to walk without it in darkness by His breath.

"I am the way, the truth and the life"

The limitations and destructive nature of our humanity has proven that we do not need another campaign, cause, or even more education to better our future. Our minds need enlightenment to a higher plane! Our hearts need recalibration, restructuring, and synergy for greater success. Our thoughts and reason for living need to be reconnected to the Source who created life, who intended the fullest extent of joy and fulfillment within this present life.

My prayer is that before you read any further, you take an uninterrupted moment to receive the breath of life ~ the rebirthing of your spirit to enable your mind to be switched on by the Holy Spirit. Remember, it is not something you can attain but something that is your inheritance by Christ's blood covenant with you.

Simply accept this redemption in the name of Jesus with a true and open heart. Then receive His illuminated heart and mind to show you the way, the truth and the life. He will not only enter your life, but also recreate it for His glory!

THE ETERNAL LIGHT

What you hear, see and experience can shape your thinking. But it doesn't mean you're supposed to have your thinking *depend solely* upon these sources.

The Scripture instructs you to renew your mind (Romans 12:1-2), which essentially means you are to realign to the original and eternal *source* of thoughts.

You might have access to the mind of the Lord but you might not be consciously connected to it. For example, a person raised in the poorest parts of Africa where people are starving, can be living in America where there is plenty ~ yet still live in lack because of a poverty mindset. Each person still has to break through into the light by switching on the mind of Christ offered to them by a relationship.

Part of breaking through into this light is getting past your own ego. "Getting ahead of yourself" has new meaning as we place the mind of Christ before our own. The mind of Christ thinks soberly according to the degree of faith God has given. It does not depend on personality, opinion or self-esteem. It depends on God's character.

Romans 12:3 (Amp)

"For by the grace [of God] given to me I say to everyone of you not to think more highly of himself [and of his importance and ability] than he ought to think; but to think so as to have sound judgment, as God has apportioned to each a degree of faith [and a purpose designed for service]."

The mind of Christ always shines outward. It regards others before the spotlight of self. Other than loving God first, truly loving people is not asking if they know Jesus before they know you, for the true Light is already active. People notice your true essence before they notice anything you are saying. Become genuinely involved with the lives of those God places before you. The eternal light will do its job without your interference in having preconceptions, prejudices or any self-serving motives.

In the meanwhile, your shining example will become the encourager of people's potential and strengths. You will be one that sincerely lets them see their value and worth from your value of eternity. It is said that "people do not remember how much you know but how you make them feel". Your inner "light on a hill" provides the illumination of the truth and the eternal image of God to the world. Without your light, people in darkness are lost, directionless, heading for danger. The presence of the Lord places a lasting and eternal impression in the subconscious heart of man.

Before long, open hearts ask you where your source of hope and love comes from. Be ready then to give your personal testimony, more than doctrine. You will be leading others in becoming eternal, light-minded, just like the Lord Jesus modeled to you.

 C380

Matthew 5:14-15 (Amp)

"You are the light of [Christ to] the world. A city set on a hill cannot be hidden; nor does anyone *light a lamp and put it under a basket, but on a lampstand, and it gives light to all who are in the house."*

CHAPTER 2
A MIND OF TRUTH

○§℃○

PSALM 51:6 (NKJV)

"Behold, You desire truth in the inward parts, and in the hidden part You will make me to know wisdom"

THE HIDDEN, SIMPLE TRUTH

Understanding more about the eternal, light-attribute of God the Holy Spirit, must be coupled with the foundational concept of eternal truth. This chapter will challenge you to not depend on your intellect to understand this concept. Surrender yourself right now to truthfully tap into the Holy Spirit and simply ask Him to help you understand this attribute of God that is vital for your spiritual growth.

With the gift of truth comes the gift of wisdom. Among the myriad of references to truth in Scripture, Jesus declared Himself to be *"the truth."* (John 14:6).

The Apostle John declared Jesus as *"...the only begotten of the Father, full of **grace and truth.**"* (John 1:14)

Focus on these two attributes of Jesus for a moment. As soon as you received the breath of God (the Holy Spirit), you were introduced to having the mindset of eternal truth. By this truth you grow in wisdom.

The Old Testament Hebrew word for "truth" is *"emet,"* which is spelled with the first, middle and last letters of the Hebrew alphabet. Thus, rabbis conclude that truth upholds the first and the last of God's creation, and everything in-between! Having a mind filled with truth is receiving your full, abundant covenant inheritance in Jesus.

God brought this about in my own life by a hidden, simply truth. It was a painful process but I am so grateful to God about it today. When I was going through the process I was perplexed and grieved. But today I stand in awe at the ways of God's Fatherhood bringing me into the truth of "sonship". My father died when I was about eleven years old and the choice to be either bitter or be content about it, was a process of unveiling grace. My father was a prominent and sweet man and losing him had a significant effect on me as a young boy.

Whilst mourning his death, I was also upset with God and with everyone ~ especially when I regarded friends who still had parents.

As time passed, the Holy Spirit brought about the acceptance of my father no longer being part of my future, and I sensed I was crossing over into another phase of life.

Then, pursuing a greater need for peace, I started seeing the truth of God's heart for me through His Word. An acceptance of this truth blossomed into the reality that God is my original father and that He will continue to take care of me and supply all my needs. This gave me an inner strength to identify and resist the mentality of an orphan. The Father's perfect love gave me a reason for living ~ a positivity, a security in the faithfulness of a caring Heavenly Father. I was permanently wearing an inner smile!

Progressively, I started realizing that God's personal truth for my individual life was a treasure to pursue. I started viewing these revelations as God's individual, prophetic voice for my life. I could hear God's voice calling me all these years beyond the ordinary to an extraordinary way of thinking ~ and thereby living. I was breaking through from having an orphan spirit that desired to give me an inability to dream. I was breaking through to have the ability to dream by the foundation of His personal, prophetic words to me ~ to keep hoping and shaping God-thoughts into my reality.

I recognized growth and transformation but it was a gradual, gentle process. As days, weeks and months sometimes dragged by, I could only embrace the tender mercy and truth of the Holy Spirit, who lead me to embrace the full truth of God's love. That security gave me an ability to not stop dreaming, hoping and expecting God's best. Instead of a lack of drive, I had supernatural faith and a vision to advance forward. It felt like I was not only viewing the kingdom of God from afar, but He was leading me to enter that place of rest. Instead of a sense of entitlement, He gave me a language of thanksgiving and praise as a king and priest. Instead of always expecting to be on the receiving-end of handouts, or comfortable with how bad life had turned out, He put me in the company of people who recognized God in my life, and the favor of God flourished. The Lord had surely been *true* to His holy Word, for He had given me the gift of wisdom.

Today, I have the faith and the hope to dream, to speak and think big because I am totally secure in a great God who calls me royalty through His Son. I am convinced of the truth that in His wisdom He has His best interests at heart for me.

Part of receiving the mind of Christ is receiving the truth of wisdom, which is not only having assurance in something, but in *someone* ~ Jesus Himself. He is the embodied word of God, who is the upholding power of our lives.

John 1:17 (NKJV)

"For the law was given through Moses, but grace and truth came through Jesus Christ"

The truth of the abiding Word of God created the mind of Christ in me, not the Law of Moses (John 8:13-36). Even though there was a time of pain, looking back today I treasure the experience of the grief of losing my earthly father, which allowed me to grasp the truth of who my true heavenly Father is!

FREEDOM FROM LIES

As I started resting in my newfound identity as a son of heaven, I started realizing that each time my self-pitying flesh wanted to return to my past identity, I lost an ability to hear God. God communicates and refers to you in the person He has created you to be ~ His emancipated son. So many Christians are stuck in religious bondage instead of true relationship with God. Jesus prayed that just as the Father regards Jesus Himself, so He wanted the Father to regard you and I. You need to have a *free* mind of truth in order to come into your full relationship and identity in the Lord.

In understanding the foundational concept of simple truth, let us compare and combine the meanings of the words "truth" in both the New and Old Testaments. The Hebrew word for truth is a derivative of the verb *"aman,"* meaning "to be firm, permanent, and established". This concept transcends the truth of the written word, which only becomes religious practice. God's true word given to you by the Holy Spirit grants you an inner humble strength, a sense of being established and preserved in your faith. This word, active in your heart and spirit, recreates you from being a person depending on intellect, being set on being law-abiding and working your spirituality through your own personality. Jesus' words, living and abiding in you, allows you to become a true follower, a disciple of truth ~ and in so doing, becoming a life-giving spirit guided into God's grace and truth. This is truth! This is freedom!

But let us not totally disregard reshaping our intellect according to the wisdom of His Word. The New Testament Greek word for truth is *"aletheia"* which means "the opposite of fictitious; feigned; false. It denotes honesty, reality, sincerity, accuracy, integrity, truthfulness, dependability, and decency." Now compare this to the Old Testament Hebrew word *"emet"* (truth). It conveys attributes of "dependability, firmness, and reliability ~ something upon which a person may confidently stake his life" (Strong's Concordance).

The Greek word for "truth" is also derived from the concept of being hidden, to escape notice. The attribute of truth in Jesus was the reason why it was appropriate for the Son of God to be born in a stable ~ inconspicuous to human eyes but conspicuously born to the true spiritual eye. In like manner, we are born of the Spirit and we live uncontested by the natural, seeing eye. We live by faith, by the Spirit and not by sight (2 Cor. 5:7).

Jesus explained His source of submission to the skeptical Pharisees in John 8:28-30. Jesus modeled the position we are to take in the mind of Christ ~ to live "under cover" of the Father alone, to be submitted directly to God. When we live in the truth, we live in the freedom of "sonship-submission" and do not judge by the flesh or depend on someone else's witness. We connect directly with the Lord as a discipline, on a daily basis, as a mature responsibility towards Him.

Jesus had discernment that those who did not know the Father would not recognize Him. Our direct connection with the Holy Spirit emancipates us from the incarceration of the law and of man's positioning, elevation or labeling. It positions us with those that truly recognize and know the Father abiding inside us.

Being submitted to the Lord also allows you to discern and dispel demonic spirits, for they do not recognize *you*, but they recognize the light of Christ in and around you. If you are totally submitted to God, they do not recognize you personally, as the "light-armor" makes you faceless and nameless. You are thus totally covered in Jesus. This proves that the light within is a life-giving ray to faith-filled minds, but it is like destructive radiation to demonic minds. The sons of Sceva (in Acts 19:13-15) were overcome by demonic forces for they did not understand authority in truth.

True "sonship-submission" (as per John 8:28-30) can be a lonely road at times but it positions you optimally with God. It should not deter your sense of being firm, fixed, permanent and established in your identity in the Lord. As you persist by faith in the ways of Jesus, in laying your life down for those whom God places in your path, your obedience will bear true fruit. Those who follow the Father will recognize you by the Spirit and not by their preference, judgment or opinion.

THE SECURITY OF TRUTH

In the freedom of the Spirit of Truth (John 14:17), we are sheltered *in* the world, yet His light in us makes us significant only to glorify the Lamb! The light emitted from us transfers our identity for His glory, so we are recognized by the light within and not by our self-righteous acts. Our relationship with the Spirit of Truth, the Holy Spirit, frees us from the religious spirit that binds us by dead rituals.

God's mind about the Spirit's abiding word in you is that He has placed His most life-giving, valued treasure inside you. You however, are invited to respond to this grace; you have the responsibility to ponder and hide His Word in your heart, like Mary did and treasure it above all else (Luke 2:19). This process brings you to a place of walking in guided maturity and submission the Lord's Fatherhood.

Having the mind of Christ, which is truth, sets you free to be totally covered by God Himself. You thereby become invisible to the enemy but totally conspicuous and precious to the Lord. But you might not understand what God's process is if you are focusing on what you see or experience. You have to renew your mind by standing on that which you *know* in your heart. Know the truth of His prevailing Word that opens your spiritual eyes to see the faith-realm of His Spirit.

John 8:31-32 (NKJV)

"Then Jesus said to those Jews who believed Him, 'If you abide in My word, you are My disciples indeed. And you shall know the truth, and the truth shall make you free'"

Freedom from fear knows the full truth about God and what He thinks of you. As a believer you are to also enter into the disciplines of the truth of the Spirit. Whenever there is need to defend the faith, a "religious spirit" knows how to distract from the main issue ~ it is always regarding the issue of truth. The word *disciple* places the emphasis on *discipline,* of being mentored. To be filled with the Spirit means you are a joyfully submitted, devoted, obedient follower, believer and supporter of Christ and His kingdom cause. You are also a joyful adherent, consistent student, scholar and learner. All of it providing increasing glory to the Lord of your life.

Soldiers are trained, first and foremost, to be a disciplined and obedient person. From this place they are enabled to engage and to combat the enemy. We are unable to wield the sword of the Spirit accurately if we are not committed to guide discipline as a fruit of the Spirit.

Soldiers use infrared vision to detect enemy forces at night. Most battles are strategized with the cloak of either fading light or darkness. This brings about great confidence in battle. The technology of infrared vision uses an invisible detector working at mid and long wavelengths to capture the heat emitted by an object. Similarly, the enlightened mind of Christ covered by the "red" blood of Jesus provides the believer the hidden, truth-filled ways of operating contrary to the enemy, and those he works through. We have discernment by the light of His truth of the father of lies, Satan. We work in ways that the enemy is unable to track or to read, since we move in two contrasting spheres of light.

As you abide in the truth of His Word, your inner self is aligned to heaven's ways. You move in dimensions of light that not only dispel darkness, but also allow you to observe and penetrate attacks and strongholds of darkness. Dominion is gained because of this supernatural discernment, and so strategizes victory by the Spirit. Victory, however, is not the eventual outcome ~ but the glory of God is.

John 3:8 (Amp)

"The wind blows where it wishes and you hear its sound, but you do not know where it is coming from and where it is going; so it is with everyone who is born of the Spirit"

God is shining His spectrum of light individually on each of us, day and night to reveal the truth of His heart and Word for our lives and nations. "Arise and shine for your light has come!"

TRUTH-FILLED WORSHIP

Now that we understand how the Holy Spirit communicates in truth, we are to also understand by the mind of Christ how to communicate in truth to *Him*. Another one of the "stealth-weapons" of grace to having the truth of God's mind, is the blessing of being covered by the Lord through your intimate times with Him, especially the daily practice of prayer and worship.

John 4:23 (NKJV)

"But a time is coming and is already here when the true worshipers will worship the Father in spirit [from the heart, the inner self] and in truth; for the Father seeks such people to be His worshipers"

In John 4, when Jesus met the Samaritan woman at the well, He was in an attitude of fasting. He was modeling the discipline of a lifestyle of dependence on God. As He requested a drink of water from her, He also had to correct an error and bring truth regarding the act of worship.

He used the natural object of water to focus on the true object of worship. He revealed Himself as the source of life. But in doing so He was also revealing the nature of the Father as the object of our worship. He explained that the Lord seeks worshippers who have an attitude of faith ("in spirit") and of transparency ("in truth").

Jesus is pointing us towards the manner of approach, or how we should relate to God. He is demonstrating that our worship and prayer must not only be in faith (seeing the invisible by the Word), but our communication is to be from a truthful heart ~transparent, sincere and according to biblical mandates. In our life of prayer, praise and conduct, our mind is to be in Christ ~ filled with the source of light, truth and abundant life. Imagine the progress in personal worship times, not neglecting to mention what corporate worship can become!

I emphasize the concept of transparency or truth in ministry. In my early days as a crusade minister in Africa I was leading a healing service. The need for people to get healed was overwhelming and I felt a spirit of intimidation and inadequacy attempting to distract me from my assignment. The desperately sick were lining up in busloads and no one was asking me permission for prayer!

As soon as I started truthfully confessing my adequacy, I felt the refreshing wind of the Holy Spirit blow through my being and I started praying in the Spirit. I could feel my heart attitude starting to shift and before long as we worshipped, a spontaneous shout erupted from my spirit: *"Jesus!"* My faith blossomed and I felt the desire to physically touch each person but the need was just too great. At the moment a "handkerchief" seemed too small, so I cast my jacket over the crowd and miraculously a whole group of people fell out under the power of God! And this was only the beginning of the service!

We do not need elaborate stage sets, sound systems and well-dressed ministers. We only need *Jesus!* He works mostly for and through the child-like, yet astounds even the greatest. I'm still hearing of the many testimonies from Africans receiving the power and the healing of the Lord from those crusade days.

Things in the Spirit are simple, and though they might seem unconventional or even weird to the natural mind, they happen in God's perfect order. Since we have "pea-sized" minds compared to His, God only requires our co-operation, humbleness and submission to just "flow" in His Spirit. Resolve to let go of the ways *you* want to serve God, and release your minuscule imaginations of how *you* think God will operate. They are insufficient in His all-sufficiency.

Rather, *really* become His follower, become His disciplined disciple to witness His glory unfolding before your very eyes. Be continually filled with the Spirit to offer worship in truth.

ACTIVATE THE DISCIPLINE OF TRUTH

People don't want to be around people that are negative or opinionated. I'm not talking about people that cannot be disciplined when they're wrong, for if someone is corrected in love it is a positive action. I'm talking about people who willfully choose to be habitually negative, who hide from the God's truth. It is a medical fact that habitual complaining programs the mind to fall into a destructive emotional and physical state. It happens one little word at a time, just like you would layer a painting, so negative words "paint" the mind with destructive ways.

We must discern between negative, destructive speaking, and correctional, uplifting speaking. I've had great people who have positively contributed in my life, who also have corrected me in love when I'm wrong.

John 3:21 (NKJV)

"But he who does the truth comes to the light, that his deeds may be clearly seen, that they have been done in God"

In the developing years of ministry a valuable friend identified ways I could improve my appearance, and advised me to always be looking my best as a kingdom representative. As a missionary-mindset tends to be independent, I didn't understand why this was necessary and felt a little offended. Years passed and this small act of love has borne fruit in how I see my life today. I know now that God spoke to him to invest in me by buying me a silky suit, leather dress shoes, a crisp shirt and tie.

God was using my friend to dress me physically so I could grow emotionally and renew my mind about how my Father sees me. Even though I was reluctantly cooperating, God took my willingness to learn to groom me for great spiritual things. God wants us to even dress and look the part He has prepared for us in Christ! The natural should manifest the spiritual!

Right now, embrace the truth about how the Father sees you. Realize how important and necessary that temporal and humble training is to prepare you for the glorious life you shall live in Christ. Be happy in this discipline and be grounded in the truth of His word, knowing that

He has prepared you to stand before kings for His Kingdom. How overjoyed, prepared and confident I felt years later when God opened a door to speak to a very prominent minister, Dr. Bruce Wilkinson.

This joy far superseded the pain of enduring the discipline of submitting to God's discipline.

My mind had been transformed and grateful that my friend didn't "mind his own business" about my attire! The Holy Spirit leads at times to not be minding our own business when we're going about the Father's business!

I will share with you one nugget I took away from this meeting with Dr. Wilkinson. As a member of one of the largest churches in America I was astounded, first of all, at how well and able he looked at his age. But the truth of his statement brought about a gratefulness of the process of discipleship I had allowed by the Father's touch. He said, "Gershom, be fully dependent upon the Holy Spirit"; and, "Always remain positive!"

Christians have forgotten how important it is, in their quest for truth, to also remain dependent upon the Holy Spirit. I believe this truth, setting you free, will always help you remain positive. Remind yourself that together we have the greatest solution to the world ~ the Holy Spirit residing in our hearts and minds. He can produce this positive energy wherever we go, so that Jesus is celebrated.

My prayer for you at the end of this chapter is that you will delve into the absolute truths of God's love for you. And that it will lead you to that truth-filled, transparent worship times in His presence. This light in you will transform your life and those you come in contact with.

As Christ in you, "the hope of glory", builds His life in you, may you be the agent of restoration. May the Spirit of truth build an atmosphere of glory and worship to Jesus. May this truth grow a greater discernment in you to stealthily occupy territories for the kingdom. May this true fountain of living water bring everlasting life to a lost and dying world.

CRISO

John 4: 13-14 (NKJV)

"...Whoever drinks of this water will thirst again, but whoever drinks of the water that I shall give him will become in him a fountain of water springing up into everlasting life"

CHAPTER 3
THE MIND OF LOVE

ᘓ80

Philippians 2:5 (NKJV)

"Let this mind be in you which was also in Christ Jesus. Who, being in the form of God, did not consider it robbery to be equal with God, but made Himself of no reputation, taking the form of a bondservant, and coming in the likeness of men"

LOVE IS LIGHT IN ACTION

The thoughts and words of God are the essence of light. But more than that, His thoughts towards you are rooted in love, which is light in action!

In various places of worship throughout the world, love has been the unending theme. Wherever He has lovingly touched the lives of countless souls, we have also had tremendous, glorious times of loving Jesus in worship of His person.

53

Where there is a hunger for the Lord, He has physically manifested Himself through individually healing and restoring spirits, souls and bodies.

Corporately, He has also manifested His angels in beams of light, which might not have been seen with our eyes ~ but curiously, has been captured on camera.

Recently there was testimony of a whole group of people who saw manifestations of colorful lights flitting throughout the building as the people were worshipping the Lord. We know this was a personal spiritual manifestation of God's love, since some people testified they did not see the lights! However, it is not so much the manifestation of the physical essence of God, but the physical evidence in people's hearts and minds that is the greatest and most glorious testimony.

John 14:21 (NKJ)

"He who has My commandments and keeps them, it is he who loves Me. And He who loves Me will be loved by My Father, and I will love him and manifest Myself to him"

Apart from all the blessed attributes declared over the disciples on the mountain, Jesus stated, *"You are the salt... you are light of the world"* (Matthew 5:13-16). As much as God places you to be a *preserving* factor *to* your world, He also places you as His light to be the *standard* for your world.

As these two attributes are rooted in His love, the preservation and standard you contribute will never be harmful or judgmental. This is a work by His Spirit and does not depend on your qualifications, but only upon your cooperation with His Spirit.

This is a work that is constantly on the move without you wanting to "will" it to happen. If you could slow down light particles, you will see that photons are constantly on the move. When light is shining, the dormancy of darkness is replaced by active, moving particles of light-energy. So are you moving, advancing and changing the things of darkness into His glorious light.

1 Peter 2:9 (NKJV)

"But you are a chosen generation, a royal priesthood, a holy nation, His own special people that you may proclaim the praises of Him who called out of darkness into His marvellous light"

In this verse the emphasis is placed on the collective force of a chosen group of people harnessing the force of light within. The light particles coming together bring forth His praise, and this glory becomes a light that dispels darkness. It is then that love manifests itself.

Science has proven that light is dual in nature. Conclusions have been made that light is both a particle and a wave. This essential theory was further evolved from electromagnetics into quantum mechanics. Einstein believed light is a particle (photon), and the flow of photons is a wave. Like our Creator, we live and operate like moving particles of light, with each individual switching on their illuminated mind in Christ. Together, we are making a wave of spiritual revival to bring about refreshing and change. Love is ultimately the glorious result.

John 1:4-5 (NKJV)

"In Him was life, and the life was the light of men. And the light shines in the darkness and the darkness did not comprehend it"

When we receive the loving Spirit of God we have the mind of Christ. We are thereby experientially and exponentially able to look into the Spirit realm and to understand Who God is and what He is doing.

Just to be sure that we have a united understanding, the love I'm referring to is the undefeatable benevolence (kindness, compassion, generosity) and unconquerable goodwill of the love of God. This love is described so well in the Greek as "agape". Jesus echoed this age-old love standard from Deuteronomy 6:5 in Matthew 22:37 and made it "command-central":

Matthew 22:37 (NKJV)

"You shall love the Lord your God with all your heart, with all your soul, and with all your strength"

Loving God above all is the basis upon which our covenant with Christ is built. The second most important command is to love others as you love yourself. To accomplish this and to do so effectively is only made possible by the indwelling, loving Spirit of Christ. It is such a powerful and perfect force that it fulfills all others laws.

LOVE THE FOUNDATION OF PRAYER

Therefore, having a mind of love is building upon the foundation God has set all things upon. This love of the Father provided Jesus the endurance to go through the crucible of the plan of salvation. From birth to death, His unbeatable connection with the Father led Him to the most significant act of love, praying for us in the face of death.

When Jesus interceded for us with blood drops of sweat (Luke 22:44) before the crucifixion, I believe He was praying His most important thoughts. I pray you will come to understand that His mind was very personally directed to you during His life, death and resurrection. If He was crucified before the foundation of the world, His thoughts towards you have been eternal in nature.

Entering the mind of Christ allows you to personally understand the very poignant account in the garden before the cross, and how they pertain to you individually.

Your complete unity with the Father was never possible until Jesus made this covenant with you by demonstrating His *love* both before and on the cross. This one act cannot really be understood if you do not also consider the events before the crucifixion, and especially His prayer for you in the garden. In those historic, dramatic events, Jesus loved you most by spending His last thoughts and words with the Father.

In John 17:15-26, Jesus prayed for you specifically. He was asking the Father that you would be protected from evil as your covenant security guarantee from the world. His prayer that the word of truth would purify you is your covenant purity guarantee. His asking that you be one with the Father as He is One with the Father is your covenant identity guarantee. He also prayed that you would receive the same glory that Jesus would receive. This is your covenant, overcoming guarantee.

He also included you with the rest of the world, through asking that your love for Him would tell the world that He is true. Jesus ended His prayer by asking the Father most importantly, *"That the love with which You loved Me may be in them, and I in them."* This love covenant has become an unbreakable bond by which you are now led to greater dimensions of His heart and mind.

The Apostle Paul is living proof of what can happen to someone who surrenders to the love of God.

He taught that this revealed God's love as the *root* of our existence. It is our bedrock, our core, that which we are grounded in (Eph. 3:17-19 and 1 Cor. 13). This irremovable basis of love in the heart is the quintessence upon which our faith and thinking is built.

Since Christ's whole existence, operation and foundation was embedded in love, it was impossible for Him to bow to the fear of death. As Christ's love has also awakened *our* hearts, it has illuminated our thinking to die to the effects of the world. When He rose from the grave He put a fire in our cold hearts and resurrected our dead minds. We were awakened to be thinking and living from the heart and not from the mind!

HAVE YOU LEARNED TO LOVE?

Have you thus learned to love? A testimony by a late prophet emphasizes the importance of love in our thinking and living. He spoke of his visit to heaven and meeting Jesus after he died in an accident. It was a miracle how he was "returned" to earth afterwards ~ that he was sent back to tell the story. This amazing experience was used of the Lord to get the prophet to hear from the Lord first-hand, the importance of His people understanding love.

After the prophet's spirit left his body, he was conveyed to a sort of reckoning place in the heavenlies with Jesus. He was standing in front of Him while positioned beside two roads operating like conveyor belts, and people were being presented to Him. The one belt, or road, was narrow and the other was broad (see Jesus' words in Matt. 7:13-14). The majority of people coming into eternity were presented to Jesus on the wide belt. They were unable to change direction or go to Jesus because whatever they caused to become their god while on earth, was what they were wrapped and trapped in. What was so astounding is that most of these people seemed oblivious about their doomed destination! They also seemed very little concerned with Jesus or even showed remorse at their demise.

The prophet described one man who had an obsession with his backyard, and so he was completely covered and trapped in the grass of his lawn. Another person worshipped money and so his body was cocooned in dollar bills. None of these people could extend their arms to Jesus to embrace or reach out to Him, even though there was a tremendous sadness in them. Whatever the people decided to spend their time with was what eventually became the clothing (or straight jacket) of their spirit person. The conveyor belt's end was at the mouth of a huge, dark chasm, which the prophet reported was the gate of hell.

Those who were positioned on the narrow conveyor belt were free to go straight to Jesus, who opened His arms to them. They seemed to melt right back into Jesus as the originator of His creation. He did, however, first ask each person if they learned to love, and each had to reply of their account. Each person had varying degrees of love, but this one thing was the qualifying factor that kept people on that narrow way and destined for the arms of Jesus.

If love is the main qualifying factor in our quest to please God, surely this one simple act is the central requirement that should define our thinking and our character as Christians. Jesus was the forerunner ~ we simply imitate His example!

THE PRAYER OF LOVE

Apart from the many more things the Lord taught Bob in heaven, He required Bob to return to earth to teach Christians to heed this one thing, "Have you learned to love?" As soon as the prophet's spirit was returned to his body the lessons of love started. Some lessons were for him personally and some were for others. As he was not completely healed of his injuries, he had to battle getting his health back, especially being dependent upon the prayers of others. He was privileged to be supported by full-time prayer intercessors, who with God's love were fervently praying for him around the clock.

He noticed that because of their prayers, his body was recovering well ~ but as soon as the intercessors were elsewhere occupied his health would be deteriorating.

The Body of Christ needs to return to the true ministry of intercession, which is agreeing with Jesus, the great Intercessor as a means of putting love in action. We need to return to this discipline firstly, as an act of worship to the Lord. In so doing we will be enabled to pray for others with the fervency that was spoken about by James, the brother of Jesus. Note in the following Scripture the emphasis on how important the mindset of love and unity in the body of believers should be:

James 5:13-16 (NKJV)

"Is anyone among you suffering? Let him pray. Is anyone cheerful? Let him sing Psalms. Is anyone among you sick? Let him call for the leaders of the church, and let them pray over him, anointing him with oil in the name of the Lord. And the prayer of faith will save the sick, and the Lord will raise him up. And if he has committed sins, he will be forgiven"

If we are truly walking in love, the unity of believers in prayer will result in whole, healed, and happy churches. Love restores trust in God and in one another. If divine healing is needed among us, why is so little emphasis being placed on the confession of sin?

More importance should be placed in today's preaching and teaching on the prominence of confessing sin, including how to handle the practice of it from both the confessor and the one receiving the confession.

Consequently, if you confess your sin privately to the Lord but the penalty of your actions is still negatively affecting the one you sinned against, private confession to them is necessary to restore unity. Public confession, however, is to be conducted in a situation where someone has caused public harm to a group of people. Likewise, parents who have sinned in front of their children, need to also confess their sin in front of them as well, not only in prayer. Confessing sin and prayer for others is therefore a means of showing the love of God. A neglect of confession of sin is partly the reason why unforgiveness brings so much defeat among Christians.

Let love prevail, and let confession of sin be a regular practice. Let prayer for one another and heartfelt forgiveness be part of our truthful worship unto God.

James 5:16 (NKJV)

"Confess your trespasses to one another, and pray for one another, that you may be healed. The effective, fervent prayer of a righteous man avails much"

TRANSCENDENT LOVE

There are so many testimonies of the magnificent love of God reaching the unlovable and unsaved of the world, for love is inexhaustible. God Himself is accomplishing this without the direct involvement of humans, although I do believe God acts by our faith-filled prayers.

Romans 5:8 (NKJV)

"But God demonstrated His own love towards us, that that while we were still sinners, Christ died for us"

A devout Muslim who was on his spiritual journeying in Mecca told one such a story. He was in the midst of making a deeper devotion to the Muslim faith, but secretly he was desperately searching for a greater reality and a personal connection with God. As he fell asleep among his fellow Muslims at the festival, Jesus surprisingly met him in a dream. The man explained Jesus in detail as a glorious light being, as He introduced Himself as the only way to the Father.

Among the many questions of his heart being answered, the feelings of despair and hopelessness left this man as Jesus stepped up to place His hand on his heart. At that, the man woke from this very vivid dream and knew this was a supernatural encounter. Despite his Muslims friends telling him he had gone crazy and that he shouldn't be talking about Jesus in such a holy place, he knew that the only thing he had to do was immediately forsake the religion and go home.

On arrival at home his family was startled and excited to hear of his spiritual encounter. But they were overwhelmingly surprised when he started telling them of his encounter with Jesus in the dream. He told them how Jesus knew his prayers and how He placed His hand on his heart, bringing so much peace and the desired fulfillment he was praying for.

As he pointed to his heart under his shirt, he noticed that a permanent discoloration on his skin had formed since the dream encounter. He realized that that was exactly where Jesus had placed His hand! This physical, loving touch of Jesus was a physical reminder that what he had experienced in the dream was a spiritual reality. It brought total conversion to him and his environment. The love of God still rescues and redeems!

With this love in mind, our response is that of awe. In light of our inadequate humanity, questioning, reasoning and complaining, God's unconditional love eclipses even His awesome signs, miracles and wonders. His love is monumental in extent but personal in application ~ we overcome limitations of our minds ~ unbelief, negativity and obscurity.

The apostles so progressively grew in their understanding of the Lord's love, not only in His eternal covenant death, but also revealing Himself to each one personally.

Paul wrote to the Corinthians by the Spirit, expounding the attributes of God's love ~ which is also the character and nature of God in *us* (1 Cor. 13:1-13). By this love we are enabled to operate in partnership with heaven by the *gifts* of the Spirit (1 Cor. 14).

Paul's first physical encounter with the Lord that led to his conversion reveals the loving heart of God for His people.

Acts 9:3-4 (NKJ)

"As he journeyed he came near Damascus, and suddenly a light shone around him from heaven. Then he fell to the ground, and heard a vice saying to him, 'Saul, Saul, why are you persecuting Me?'"

The love of God has a way to reach a person that needs no human intervention. On the way to Damascus, Saul (who became the Apostle Paul), met up with the fervent love of God for His church ~ which took him on a fourteen-year preparatory journey. I believe the love of God is what compelled him to risk his life and start preaching the message of Christ to the Gentiles.

During this time Paul's mind, schooled under the greatest minds of the time, was renewed ~ changed and equipped through his heart renewed by love. He was given a mind of understanding of the extent of Christ's love, that it is not limited to the Jewish or the chosen nation, as was believed. He realized that tradition and made-made laws had formed a corrupted view of God and that the Lord was equipping him personally to extend His true nature to the entire world, regardless of nationality or race.

As we study the revelations of Paul we witness not only the process of a transformed man, but also the journey of how he received the mind of Christ ~ even concluding that His immeasurable love could be *grasped* through the mind of Christ. He spoke about the fullness of Christ, His love, having unfathomable dimensions of height, length, depth and breadth (Eph. 3:18). The love of Christ may thus attain the highest achievements, span the extent of a lifetime, reach you in the depths of hellish experiences, and even extend the breadth of eternity.

By the mind of Christ John could expound a tremendous revelation of Christ over an extended period of time. "The beloved disciple", who was part of Jesus' inner circle, wrote all the Gospels of John and the book of Revelation. He was known to be the one leaning against the breast of Jesus. The unique writings of John also reveal, through his intimacy with God, a deeper knowledge of the Holy Spirit in His designation as "Comforter", or "Helper", and "Advocate".

Beloved, as we delve into the mind of the love of God, we gain access to the greater depths of His mysteries, even beyond what the apostles and disciples received. Eternity is not sufficient to know all the dimension of the character and attributes of the Lord.

In being invited into the mind of Christ, you are inevitably invited into the mind of love.

COLD LOVE

Jesus spoke an end-time warning about how cold love can grow. Once we disregard or do not make much of the law of love, we step out of being able to proclaim the enduring Gospel needed for these end-times.

Matthew 24:12 (NKJ)

"And because lawlessness will abound, the love of many will grow cold"

A well-known teacher in America recently felt led of the Lord to start ministering around the well-known subject of the love of God. Despite thousands of books already written about love, she started writing her most profound book. However, she was astounded to learn at her book launch, that although it was her most compelling book, it sold the least.

Isn't this a good indication of how our human nature avoids or even rebels against the very attribute and nature of God that we as Christians are most encouraged to receive? Leaders need to keep making the main thing the *main* thing! If there is ever a necessity to renew the minds of believers, it has to, and *must*, start with God's love.

Wherever there has been failure, incompetence, ignorance, lack or poverty ~ you can be assured that the lack or break down of pure love started the process. Jesus recognized this when He endured aggressive opposition from the Jews who opposed the healing of the man at the Pool of Bethesda, because of it being the Sabbath day. They were incapable of receiving the gift of God and celebrate the miracle of life, not because they were abiding by the law, but because they had excluded the love of God from their devotion. And because of that they missed out on receiving life from Jesus, receiving His Word and finding the Father Himself (John chapter 5).

The theme of love will be an ever-increasing and more urgent subject in these end-times. The subject of love will never go out of date and can never be emphasized enough since it is the central point in the mind of God.

If you desire to know the mind of Christ, pursue love.

ACTIVATE THE MIND OF LOVE

Our eternal *covenant* of love in Jesus has given us complete access to the mind of God ~ it is the natural progress of maturity in our relationship with Him. Just like a married couple progresses in communication, we cannot limit our spiritual maturity by being satisfied with only the joy and the warmth of His presence. We have to advance by really learning to inquire into His mind ~ and so live by it.

This also means His mind reaches your physical synapses. If you think you are unable to absorb all sixty-six books of the Bible and remember all the words of Jesus, you are not only limiting yourself but you are limiting God. There are many accounts of people who are naturally forgetful, but who can easily and promptly remember Scripture. As you remove the limits you have placed upon your mind and open up yourself to the capacity of love God wants to give you by His Spirit, the possibilities in Him are endless.

You are now not only reading the Bible as a ritual, but at each sitting you are accepting the loving invitation of the Author into your heart. You are expectant to be receiving His expounded treasures to you. You commit to being an obedient student of His Word as a lifestyle, allowing your love for the Word to grow. You are not anxious about reciting Scriptures right away, for your memory is not what impresses God; it is your desire to unite in love with Him.

All the while you are reminded of His thoughts as you choose pockets of peace throughout the day ~ opening your heart and mind to receive that still small voice, those promptings, that inner intuition. You are delighted to experience His genuine interest in building an intimate and personal connection with each one of us ~ regardless of our inabilities, weaknesses, laziness, issues, and stages of life.

I declare over your life that you are becoming mature in the Lord by love. I pray that in this way you are not only engaging in a life enhancing activity but you will recognize it vital for life. I see you taking this avenue towards breakthrough thinking in every area of your daily life. I pray that you will realize that this is a life-saving commitment, a connection that will bring His saving grace into your life and the lives of your family and nation.

I declare that Christ's rulership and kingdom is granted to be manifest through you, and that it will start with your enlightened mind.

Philippians 2:5 (NKJV)
"Let this mind be in you which was also in Christ Jesus. Who, being in the form of God, did not consider it robbery to be equal with God, but made Himself of no reputation, taking the form of a bondservant, and coming in the likeness of men"

Although Jesus had an eternal attribute as the Son of God, He didn't bother Himself with worrying about His reputation. The only reputation He was concerned about was to serve His Father and us in love. Throughout the history of time, whoever has adopted this attitude of Jesus, the love of God has been inexhaustible. You become eternal when you adopt the mindset of love.

Amidst a broken and corrupt world hurtling towards its demise, the love of God stands eternally, upholding all! If there ever was a central point within the mind of Christ, then the love of God within the story of the cross holds its epicenter. Once we allow our hearts to be captured and overcome by this love, our natural minds get translated to the supernatural, all-encompassing and incomprehensible mind of Christ! Nothing will be impossible to us. The extent of His love is portrayed in His passion for His creation. For God did not spare His most beloved Son to restore the love connection He desires to have with each of us.

ᐒᑍ

CHAPTER 4
COVENANT MIND

C880

Hebrews 4:14

"Seeing then that we have a great High Priest who has passed through the heavens, Jesus the Son of God, let us hold fast our confession"

THE ACCESS OF AGREEMENT

Having full access to the heavens is an understanding reserved for each believer. Our Champion, Jesus, made this possible. If you have access to someone's life, you have access to his or her mind. Sin and the law divided us from this access, but Jesus *"passed through the heavens"* ~ He broke through the heavens on our behalf to give us full access through the dividing veil and gave us perfect access and understanding of Father God.

In order to understand access fully, we must search into the mind of God concerning the sacrificial covenant through Jesus Christ. The word "covenant" is an agreement, promise or pledge. We have the mind of Christ to be in agreement with the heavens. Have you noticed that close family members have developed an intuition in knowing what each is thinking or going to say? Even on a closer level, a married couple that has a close covenant relationship seeking the will of God, often go aside separately to hear from God. Many times, after getting together again to hear what each received from God, they get the confirmation from the Lord by the two words agreeing to one will.

This is accomplished by the promise of the Holy Spirit. Despite the many trails and tribulations within our privileges, He is our guarantee that what we know is truly eternal in nature, that our covenant is real and lasting.

2 Corinthians 5:4-5 (NKJV)

"For we who are in this tent groan, being burdened, not because we want to be unclothed, but further clothed, that mortality may be swallowed up by life. Now He who has prepared us for this very thing is God, who also has given us the Spirit as a guarantee"

ACCESS TO PHYSICAL BREAKTHROUGH

Hebrews 4:14 reveals that Jesus the High Priest *"passed through the heavens",* which reveals He entered a dimension previously off limits. What Jesus accomplished for you and I was a breakthrough intervention of God. There was a veil, or curtain, placed between the holy place where people worshipped God and where God actually manifested Himself. When Jesus completed the sacrifice on the cross, the physical veil tore in two (Matt. 27:51), but that was only the result of the spiritual gap that was broken down. This means we not only escaped death in His presence, but we could have access to God Himself. God was able to come into the physical realm and indwell our bodies as His temple! Meditate a moment upon the miracle of this taking place. This is the power of the cross; this is the understanding you need to have concerning your covenant with God!

In vast contrast to what Jesus accomplished as the sacrificed Lamb of God, studies of the Old Testament show that their sacrifices were *"dead works"* (Heb. 9:14), and thus proves that not even the highest form of righteous living is comparable to what the sacrifice and work of Jesus achieved. The only reason God instituted the Old Testament priesthood in the first place, was for it to point to the only perfect Great High Priest ~ Jesus Christ. He was, and is, the only spotless Lamb of God who would fulfill all the requirements of the law for the full redemption and salvation of souls.

Hebrews 1:3b (Amp)

"When He [Himself and no other] had [by offering Himself on the cross as a sacrifice for sin] accomplished purification from sins and established our freedom from guilt, He sat down [revealing His completed work] at the right hand of the Majesty on high [revealing His Divine authority]"

Jesus sacrificed Himself so you could have full access not only to heaven, but so heaven could come to earth! *"Purification of sins"* and *"established our freedom"* (Heb. 1:3), is His primary covenant accomplishment. Our understanding should be that we *belong* in the throne room ~ we have been "upgraded" positionally, and in status! His purification work in our heart, mind and body allows **us total access** to the throne of God.

Therefore, we can walk in an open and honest relationship with the Lord, coming *"boldly to the throne of grace"* (Heb. 5:14-16). We should pray not in arrogance or in pride, but in a humble thankfulness of truly understanding the accomplishment of Christ in and through us.

FRIENDSHIP WITH GOD

The restoration plan of God is already complete, but our minds have to progressively come in line with the original intent of God's thinking.

In covenant with Christ there are also secrets in our relationship with God because He regards His lovers as His friends (John 15:13-14).

Earlier we discussed the way truth is established in our hearts ~ it is a hidden, stealth-like process that God works in us. And He will surely complete what He has started.

Ministers who have been in that occupation for years, regardless of being full or part time, find that placing an emphasis on *working* for God creates burnout. Becoming a friend of God is also *knowing* His mind, providing you the wisdom to be passionately in love with Him without suffering burnout!

Just as there is an intimate life away from the world between man and wife, so Christ requires His Bride to offer service only to Him and not for recognition or praise. In Matthew 11:28, Jesus invites us into daily partnership, to unburden religious, virtual and ritual practices ~ and to really yoke with Him like two oxen ploughing. He declared:

> *"Take My yoke upon you and learn from Me [following Me as My disciple], for I am gentle and humble in heart, and you will find rest (renewal, blessed quiet) for your souls."* (Amp)

Notice Jesus' metaphor of the ploughing oxen in gaining an understanding of how He builds relationship with us. The reference is illustrating a relationship being formed while walking or being active together in life. As I mentioned before regarding receiving the breath of life, allow the Lord to teach you how to breathe, to instruct you how to live!

It is not always waiting for an opportune time or a quiet space where we connect with God, which is still good. But for many of us, our lives and work also need to be intentionally yoked together with Jesus even while engaging menial tasks. He wants to clothe, or bond you to Himself to provide you with all you need. This personal presence will not necessarily bring you out of problems or challenges, but it most certainly will lead you *through* them.

A friend of mine was telling me about her occupation in the design industry. As she was working long and unusual hours, it occupied her mind to such a degree that she didn't notice a gradual diversion from her devotion to the Lord. She systematically started walking outside of the rhythms of grace. Her family was both annoyed and traumatized by how this trapped her in an emotional vortex and brought her to the brink of collapse. It happened in repeated cycles to such a degree that she finally had to totally dislodge herself from the industry and pursue doing something else for a while in order to refocus her mind on the important things in life. She had simply focused so much on the job at hand through pride and fear, that she got herself "unyoked" with Jesus as Friend.

I pray you will have the wisdom to know immediately what to forfeit in order for your soul to be saved, for He desires for us to in close friendship ~ living freely and lightly.

Matthew 16:26 (NKJV)

"For what profit is it to a man if he gains the whole world, and loses his own soul? Or what will a man give in exchange for his soul?"

His Word is focused on ways of drawing you to becoming His closest friend. In His gentleness He is fully committed by covenant to your decision to cultivate your mind as healthy and vibrant ground for Him to sow seeds of promise and newness of life.

Notice in The Message translation how Jesus' invitation places emphasis on the proximity and pace we share with Jesus. We are matching His strength in bearing forward, but His Spirit is continually focusing forward, moving ahead. It always has an advancing motion. But it is also sensitive to your humanity and limitations ~ He is freely showing you how to rest, how to walk and work without forcing you. Living freely and lightly with Him is His intention for you.

Matthew 11:28 (MSG)

"Are you tired? Worn out? Burned out on religion? Come to me. Get away with me and you'll recover your life. I'll show you how to take a real rest. Walk with me and work with me—watch how I do it. Learn the unforced rhythms of grace. I won't lay

anything heavy or ill-fitting on you. Keep company with me and you'll learn to live freely and lightly"

Your life or career might be like that over-laden camel that is restricted from going forward through the "narrow" gate as a result of his burden.

In ancient times the entrances to cities were designed for security so that only the camel without baggage could fit through the entrance. That way suspect baggage could be identified.

See Jesus as the only way, the only door, and the only gate towards liberty. That which we treasure most at times seems to be the very thing withholding us from the only way, the truth and the life. The *"eye of the needle"* (Matthew 19:24), which was known in ancient times as the narrow gate, could only be entered if the camel knelt down and had all his baggage unburdened. It is worth kneeling before Jesus, allowing Him to unburden all those religious yokes ~ to live for Him in the freedom of friendship.

The Lord desires true friendship with you ~ a vibrant relationship by which you collaborate in the gift of life with Him. You were designed for communion with God.

What He is revealing or giving you now is not always primarily *about* you, but about the greater good He has designed *through* your life. Meditate upon the thoughts of the Lord ~ that He is *for* you! There will then be no room for inferior thinking, and soon your faith will grow to a rock-solid knowing that He can do so much through you for the advantage of others.

Start valuing your mind as a place where you meet God as your best friend ~ a holy habitation where God dwells to affect your world.

As His mind gets transferred to yours, God's energy will start cascading through your life. Allow Him to do His complete will through your talents, innovations, business, and discoveries. God wants to deposit countless supernatural things to you ~ so give yourself the freedom of intimate times with Him to develop these things in the light of God's purpose.

Psalm 139:17 (TLB)

"How precious it is, Lord, to realize that You are thinking about me constantly! I can't even count how many times a day Your thoughts turn toward me. And when I waken in the morning, You are still thinking of me!"

BY HIS SPIRIT

Making Jesus' friendship a priority in your life, discovering His mind on a daily basis, and allowing the Lord to nourish and sustain you ~ brings you to the limitless resources of His mind, intentions and plans for your life.

Jesus proclaimed Himself to be the *"I Am"*, which makes Him the sole provider of our spirits, souls and bodies. In John 4:14 He is the Living Water for our thirst. In John 6:34 He is the Bread of Life for our hunger. In John 10 He is the Good Shepherd for our straying hearts. And in John 15 He declares Himself to be the Vine for our need to belong.

No amount of books, sermons, DVDs, videos or conferences can really provide this full, personal, unique nourishment you need as you intentionally worship, connect and learn from Him at each sunrise. The other things are only to reinforce your time with Him.

Like the branches of a natural vine, we cannot produce anything without our vital connection to the Vine, to receive and live by that unbreakable bond (John 15). This bond is offered to us in the form of the eternal shed blood of Jesus, the covenant love of Jesus shown to all mankind on the cross.

Because Jesus gave His life, we can no longer tolerate spiritual malnourishment and remain mediocre thinkers that produce mediocre lives. We have to return to the true authority that the Father intended, the daily submission of our wills conformed to His mind.

May our prayers return to the prayer of Jesus, *"Let Your kingdom come, let Your will be done on earth as it is in heaven"* (Matt. 6:10). Even though Jesus was the Son of God and vitally connected with Him, He still had to seek the will of His Father who is the source of all authority. Once we desire the will of the Father above all, we no longer desire things from our own initiative. Synonyms for initiative are plan, scheme, idea or program. May our inventiveness come from the resourcefulness of the mind of Christ.

John 5:30 (Amp)

"I can do nothing on My own initiative or authority. Just as I hear, I judge; and My judgment is just (fair, righteous, unbiased), because I do not seek My own will, but only the will of Him who sent Me"

God would never have had an interest in creating the universe if He didn't have an interest in man, and therefore an interest in our thoughts. God is a lover of people and of His creation. He created both the visible and the invisible for our benefit and therefore you are inseparable in spirit, soul and body. You can accomplish your earthly assignment only by the assistance of the indwelling Spirit of God.

Zechariah 4:6

"'Not by might nor by power, but by My Spirit,' says the Lord"

THE BONDING OIL

The primary reason we have been given the mind of Christ is so our *souls* can be made one with God. Therefore, the most important reason that you were given the wisdom of Christ is to *choose* God first! The smartest thing you can do is keep the synergy of your mind in sync with the Holy Spirit each day. Just like the priests had to daily replenish the oil of the lampstand in the holy place, so we are to refresh our connection with the Lord each day.

The symbol of oil has always related to the presence and the Spirit of God. The parable of the ten virgins in Matthew 25 is a picture of the end-time church that wisely chooses to replenish their faithfulness to God through their growing partnership with the Holy Spirit. Though the foolish virgins were faithful, not only did they forget to get oil but didn't have the inner intuition of the time of Christ's return. The vital connection with God will give you longevity and vision for the timing of the last days before His return.

From the same parable we can also deduce that our bond with the Holy Spirit makes us distinct, and recognizable to God. The virgins having their lamps trimmed and burning enabled them to enter the Bridegroom's chamber. This prophetic Scripture lists the attributes the Holy Spirit provides as the mind of Christ:

Isaiah 11:1-2 (NKJV)

"There shall come forth a Rod from the stem of Jesse, and a Branch shall grow out of His roots. The Spirit of the Lord shall rest upon Him, the Spirit of wisdom and

understanding, the Spirit of counsel and might, the Spirit of knowledge and of the fear of the Lord"

In the same way Jesus' practical ministry started when He received the Holy Spirit, your connection with God and mind transformation started at that event. It didn't start when you went to church, listened to sermons, or read the Bible ~ for the word of God only becomes effective by the indwelling Holy Spirit. When you received the supernatural infilling it caused a supernatural regeneration of your spirit and mind and started transforming your world.

Through His anointing and empowerment Jesus was *enabled* to fulfill Scripture through the Spirit of wisdom, understanding, counsel, might, knowledge and the fear of the Lord. He was thus able to *pray* in the will of God, *"Not my will, but Yours, be done"* (Luke 22:43). He was able to commune with the Father apart from His natural will.

Similarly, your spirit and mind is now in synergy with heaven. You have His discernment and you have His intuition. You have prophetic foresight and you are able to be in submission to do the will of the Father. Your emotions are in sync with the Holy Spirit and your intellect is washed, renewed and super-boosted!

Not only do you have all these benefits but also you have an inner security, a crazy peace that you belong, you are never alone and that you have an incredible destiny. The peaceful, loving presence of the Holy Spirit is the eternal guarantee that all these things are absolute truth!

When the Spirit of God is leading you, you sense the joy of His presence, and His mind becomes your mind. You can even sense the mind of God and know what God is thinking. It is so wonderful that the mind of God can be ours! This can happen when you allow the Holy Spirit to lead your life. He is the oil of joy that keeps our spirits bonded to His.

Matthew 25:10-12 (NKJV)

"And while they went to buy, the bridegroom came, and those who were ready went in with him to the wedding; and the door was shut.

"Afterward the other virgins came also, saying, 'Lord, Lord, open to us!' But he answered and said, 'Assuredly, I say to you, I do not know you."

಼ಌ

PART 2
RENEWING THE MIND

CHAPTER 5
RENEWED THINKING

ೞ

Romans 12:1-2 (NKJ)

"I beseech you therefore, brethren, by the mercies of God, that you present your bodies a living sacrifice holy acceptable to God, which your reasonable service. And do not be conformed to this world, but be transformed by the renewing of your mind, that you may prove what is that good and acceptable and perfect will of God"

The only way our bodies are an acceptable sacrifice is through the active demonstration of love on a daily basis. As you choose love in every decision and in each activity, you are appropriately representing not only yourself as sons of God, but presenting the tangible love of God. Having your mind renewed by the love of God is the perfect will of God for your life.

Think of the possibilities of transformation happening in your life and the lives of others! Love nurtures every part of our existence in spirit, soul and body.

PROGRESSIVE, NOT INSTANT

Accept the fact that the mind of Christ is God's work of love in progress. Like a master designer or artist, He is preforming a *perfect* work in you. Together with your spirit being renewed, your mind is being cleaned up by the power of God's word. You realize that you are completely covered and backed up in each decision and path in life. You have been created for guaranteed success!

Be aware, but don't be anxious about Satan, who might try his tactics to get to divert to condemnation or guilt ~ even reminding you that your past is very much still alive. Since Jesus already won complete victory for you, during times of testing or temptation is when your identity in Christ has to be bravely confessed by faith in Christ.

The following Scripture explains this process:

1 John 5:20 (Amp)

"And we [have seen and] know [by personal experience] that the Son of God has [actually] come [to this world], and has given us understanding and insight so that we may [progressively and personally] know Him who is true; and we are in Him

who is true—in His Son Jesus Christ. This is the true God and eternal life"

No matter your age or your stage in life, the grace of God allows you to always start over again. God is continually training you, so if you haven't managed to pass a character test ~ you get to write it until you pass! His grace is sufficient for you! As long as you have breath in your lungs, you have the power of the resurrected Christ in your life.

God is so excellent at recreating you, but your commitment to thinking as He does is your key to that freedom. Do not waste time worrying about your past once you've released it in repentant confession before the Lord. If you can get your mind to understand how your sin is grieving the heart of God and the heart of loved ones, you are in a road of changing deeply. If you can start meditating on His infallible love for you and the price He paid to prove that to you, you are on the road of great recovery!

Spend your time on what God wants to do for you today, and marvel at the countless loving thoughts He has towards you (Psalm 139). Now, who can you inspire, and who can you help with such thoughts? It is very important that you have purpose through knowing God's plan, as the enemy cannot stop this. Just have the mind that you will make it *with* Him, and that you will fulfill His dream in your heart.

Even in the midst of a resistant storm, the power to get out of it is available to you (1 Cor. 10:13).

THINKING WITH JESUS

Start speaking life today ~ whatever your situation may be. There is a God in heaven that has made all things available to you, and one of them is thinking like Jesus. What do I mean by that? It is not only taking your own thoughts to Him in hopeful prayer, but also taking the time to receive His thoughts and intuition. In this process, you are kind of exchanging thoughts ~ things like, "Should I go for this-or-that business deal? Or "Is this the right spouse for me?" Take some time out in the day where you will not be distracted, and hear from Him concerning your life.

I call this process "thinking with Jesus" which is thinking with the light of God in my life, thinking with the Word of God, through His nature and through His love. It is thinking through His power ~ knowing He is *able* to do all things. I have the dauntless freedom to dream and hope for Him to extend my capacity, making the invisible, visible!

John 16:33 (Amp)

"I have told you these things, so that in Me you may have [perfect] peace. In the world you have tribulation and distress and suffering, but be courageous [be confident, be undaunted, be filled with joy]; I have

overcome the world. [My conquest is accomplished, My victory abiding]"

HAPPINESS VERSUS JOY

Once I was suffering a relational challenge with a person, where it became necessary for a period of separation in our relationship. Even though it was painful, it was God's will for our paths to separate. Through it all I realized that God had to completely weigh my heart in the process. I was amazed how the condition of my heart was revealed at a random public place where this person happened to walk by. (It was, of course, a set-up by God, and thankfully I realized it.)

It would have been a lot more comfortable for me to ignore the person, but I chose to show love. There is a way to think ~ loving, smiling and giving ~ that activates happiness in your mind.

Happiness comes from *happenings* ~ which don't provide *lasting* happiness like joy does. Have the mindset of the joy of knowing the Lord at all times, despite reasons for fear or negativity. Such mindsets cloud your atmosphere, and can be felt by others wherever you go. A lack of knowledge causes us to perish (Hos. 4:6), so allow the Holy Spirit to develop an open mindset towards all people from all walks of life ~ no matter if your paths have to separate. To be successful and prosperous is a product of a renewed mind and a healthy spirit. Your life can be a sweet-smelling fragrance of Christ wherever you go!

Ephesians 5:1 (NKJV)

"Therefore be imitators of God as dear children. And walk in love as Christ also has loved us and given Himself for us an offering and a sacrifice to God for a sweet-smelling aroma"

Enjoy the presence of the Lord in your life. The minute you begin to lose your thanksgiving and joy, you lose peace of mind. Keep monitoring the peace and joy level in your life to know what is in your heart.

EMBRACE HEART-POSITIVITY

Thinking like Christ is more than having a positive mind. It is not just about your conscious thoughts but also more about your subconscious mind ~ which is your heart.

As God communicates through your heart, He is speaking to your spirit, which is the real, flawless, *you* in Christ. That is why we should earnestly heed subconscious dreams and visions when we are unable to apply wisdom or make difficult decisions. I will speak more about this in continuing chapters.

Negative thinking in the light of Christ isn't even an issue! You will be amazed how, as you discover the effervescent thoughts of the Lord, you will develop a sense of humor towards the attempts the enemy launches your way!

Eventually you will be able to instinctively stand strong in the Lord as you set your mind on His thoughts. I believe David acquired this habit, and the thoughts of the Lord became deep and meaningful songs to God.

Psalm 59 is a Michtam (golden Psalm) of David when Saul sent men to watch his house in order to kill him. But after each description of his reality, he directs His thoughts to what God is doing. Verse 8 reads:

> *"But You, I Lord, shall laugh at them; You shall have all the nations in derision. I will wait for You, O You my Strength; for God is my defence. My God of mercy shall come to meet me; God shall let me see my desire on my enemies"*

Then, in verse 16, David resorts to singing to the Lord in the midst of his enemies growling like dogs, pacing up and down to hunt for his flesh:

> *"But I will sing of Your power; Yes, I will sing aloud of Your mercy in the morning; for You have been my defence and refuge in the day of my trouble"*

Just like your conscious mind, your subconscious is ineffective until it is educated or stimulated. It is your responsibility to build your conscious mind based on the worship of the Cornerstone, the Rock, which is Christ Jesus Himself (Matthew 7:24). When Jesus declared He would build His church upon this Rock, He didn't mean building a structure on earth. He meant our connection and revelation of Him, brings us to brighter and smarter ways of doing things. We then become immovable and unshakeable.

What thoughts are you thinking about yourself? What image are you building? What you build upon will determine what you become. These thoughts should be an agreement of what God is thinking of you ~ the positive, life-giving Word of God. Through much intentional, conscious and meditational thinking, the Word of God becomes the subconscious and sinks into your heart through the indwelling work of the Holy Spirit.

The Message translation gives us more insight into the process of renewing the mind. The outcome of this co-operation with the Lord is so we are prepared to enter and walk in a relationship with Lord as the mature bride of Christ.

Romans 12:2 (NKJV)

"So here's what I want you to do, God helping you: Take your everyday, ordinary life—your sleeping, eating, going-to-work, and walking-around life—and place it

before God as an offering. Embracing what God does for you is the best thing you can do for Him.

Don't become so well-adjusted to your culture that you fit into it without even thinking. Instead, fix your attention on God. You'll be changed from the inside out.

Readily recognize what He wants from you, and quickly respond to it. Unlike the culture around you, always dragging you down to its level of immaturity, God brings the best out of you, develops well-formed maturity in you.

CR80

CHAPTER 6
ACTIVATING YOUR MIND

ೲ

Hebrews 1:6 (NKJV)

"But without faith it is impossible to please Him, for he who comes to God must believe that He is, and that He is a rewarder of those who diligently seek Him"

THE SPARK OF LOVE

Your breakthrough mind in Christ is inherited but it must remain activated by the dynamic *use* of faith. In the same way you could grow overweight by little activity or physical exercise and so not fully use the positive energy of food, so we can become sluggish in faith that remains dormant. Faith can therefore become harmful if it is not practical, turning into religiosity.

Faith is indeed a broad subject but the essence of it is that the mind of Christ within your spirit-person operates by your trust in God's character and His unchangeable nature. Your active relationship with the Holy Spirit energizes and brings the dynamics of faith into being. Faith is the mindset of heaven operating in your natural mind. It is the principle by which the physical is impacted by the spiritual.

In your personal walk with God, His love will always remain that vibrant flame by which you live your life. It is the conduit of faith. Once you realize God's amazing love for you personally, your faith in Him grows ~ and that is where the realm of God's reward comes into being. God is the epitome of generosity and kindness. He grants you the fuel of the heavenlies by which love is released in the natural. Your motive, therefore, in activating your mind of faith in love, is using the conduit by which the love of God in the earth is released. In so doing His kingdom is made manifest, He receives the glory, and your needs are met.

We understand that God, who is love, created everything by the word of His mouth (Heb. 11:3). Notice the emphasis on our dependence of God Himself as the fuel of our faith. Faith is therefore living to love God, walking by the discernment and the intuition of His Spirit. This is quite a mouthful, so let's look at The Message translation regarding the subject of how faith relates to love and how grace undergirds it all.

Galatians 5:4- 6 (MSG)

"...When you attempt to live by your own religious plans and projects, you are cut off from Christ, you fall out of grace. Meanwhile we expectantly wait for a satisfying relationship with the Spirit. For in Christ, neither our most conscientious religion nor disregard of religion amounts to anything. What matters is something far more interior: faith expressed in love"

MEDIOCRE TO EXTRAORDINARY

Just like the replenishing oil of the Holy Spirit activates us spiritually, so the Word of God builds our faith. Unbelief is mediocre thinking and it is therefore an abuse of redemption. We are supposed to be in that place of overcoming faith by maintaining trust in Jesus.

A friend of mine was suffering from low esteem and it caused a crippling of his mind and he wasn't being himself. I sensed from his body language and melancholy attitude that his thoughts were negative. He was losing focus for a while and his courage to advance in the Lord got affected.

As we conversed about his situation, he confessed what was actually bothering him ~ he had lost hope to believe for a godly wife. Through disappointments and delays he had

99

come to the conclusion that he didn't deserve to be loved.

I encouraged his faith by urging him to have courage like David ~ to worship and wait upon the Lord and trust Him with all his heart. That seemed to calm him down and before long his courage and hope returned. As soon as he started relaxing and believing in God, not focusing on the girl but on His God, the breakthrough came. God provided a wife that superseded his expectation ~ but matched His faith in God.

All along, despite my friend's doubting mindset, God's mind about a life partner for him was superseding his own dream for a wife. The love and acceptance he received from the Lord, demonstrated through his wife, totally restored his self-esteem bringing him to a secure identity in the Lord.

When the Lord provides, it always restores value and builds the heart and vision. This friend realized he was undermining his potential because of the mindset he had formed through his past. Know that only the mind of God knows the future, and so we tap into His prophetic knowing while acting upon His word. It is wise to trust Him without reserve and to expect the best. For that is His will for your life.

Stay positively true to the Lord's word by faith, even though your world might be flooded with the negativity of bad experiences and the misery of failure. Do not be the one to *add* to the misery, but be the one to add *hope* and *love* and expectation of good things to happen.

Find your sense of purpose and destiny by hearing His voice in the "closet of prayer". Delve even deeper through sound preaching and teaching. You will always have a progressive mind and a great future!

Romans 10:17 (Amp)

"So faith comes from hearing [what is fold], and what is heard comes by the [preaching of the] message concerning Christ"

With a hunger for His Word, His gifts and talents within, you will always enhance both your relationships and your environment. His greatness will manifest as you determine to keep your mind focused on Jesus. His love confirms that you are a gift to the earth and His Spirit within will always give you the victory because He has overcome the world.

GRACE IN FAITH

Sometimes no matter what we do, our faith is not receiving breakthrough. A testimony that His grace is sufficient, even in our deficient faith, came from a woman who was listening to our Friday night Fire meetings online. She was listening intently from the West Indies, when suddenly an angel appeared in her room! God sometimes sends supernatural means to confirm His word that grants you that irrevocable conviction that what He said is what He will do.

When all else fails concerning activating faith, God can send a supernatural angelic intervention.

From Unlimited Grace in Glendale, a woman working in the medical profession was listening to one of my sermons and started practicing what was taught. From hearing the teaching tracks in the hospital, a patient was healed from a terrible sickness. She continues to minister healing by the power of having her mind renewed in Christ.

Someone else started listening to my sermons and was inspired to "dig into" the Presence of the Lord. As soon as she started listening and praying ~ signs, wonder, miracles, and heavenly visitations began to manifest in her life for several days.

All glory to Jesus who opens our spiritual ears and eyes to know Him! This is your inheritance.

DEMOLISHING UNBELIEF

If you can change your thinking, you will change your life. Take courage and increase your capacity to believe God by stretching yourself past what feels comfortable to your flesh and emotions. You will discover God's possibilities in you. No one can help you find this treasure of wisdom but you. Use your mind to contribute. Do not wait for someone else to lead or initiate. You have everything within the mind of Christ to enable you to be a great success and bring about an eternal legacy.

Start confessing His mind today in faith. Use the word of God in your private times with Him. You have to *hear* yourself agreeing with God. It reinforces your heart. Start using your mouth as that creative means through which God will do His will. Start stepping out actively in that which the Lord has placed in your heart.

I've also found great advantage in making myself available to preach and teach the revelatory word of God ~ it not only builds my personal faith but unlocks dormant faith in others. In so doing, the mind of Christ operating through me is a weapon in His hand that refutes any argument that God will not be true to His word. It humbly demonstrates love where the pride of religion wants to insist on selfish motives. It displays the irrefutable wisdom of the Spirit where ignorance and lies want to build a stronghold.

The mind of Christ through the Word of God takes unbelieving thoughts captive and does not allow them to wander towards introspection. The moment we focus on ourselves, unbelief steps in. Obedience to the word of God is a demolition process against unbelief.

2 Corinthians 10:5 (NIV):

"We demolish arguments and every pretension that sets itself up against the knowledge of God, and we take captive every thought to make it obedient to Christ."

Pretense is a spirit of unbelief, a deception, and an imagination ~ something aimed at being embedded in the mind through the pride of unbelief. When a mental picture is taken of a fearful imagination, it becomes a destructive stronghold that affects your perception, your way of thinking and manner of doing. It is the basis on which either human or demonic ways of thinking can grow.

If you choose not to confess the word of God spoken over your life, you are siding with unbelief. Since faith alone pleases the Lord, it aligns you with heavenly and not the earthly way of thinking. Refuse to be in deception, to be in opposition with heaven, and receive the way godly faith forms in your mind. There is a way of thinking that is right in *your* own mind but it won't lead you anywhere.

Proverbs 14:12 (AMP)

"There is a way which seems *right to a man* and *appears straight before him, but its end is the way of death"*

ALL-THINGS-POSSIBLE IN WORDS

When we embrace the realm of faith-filled Word-meditation and communion with God, we enter into the Lord's mindset of *"nothing is impossible"* (Mark 10:27). Through this mind of faith, the Word of God becomes alive and active and has the ability to change our hearts and create new environments.

It is therefore possible, by faith, to reject every imagination and deception that is not of God, including those thoughts that come from your independent way of thinking.

To "cast out" an unbelieving thought is also getting rid of independent and lying thoughts. It is to receive the mind of Christ to combat that thought. There is always a way out to the way in ~ so stay connected to His Spirit and to His Word, to hold captive the thoughts of God and to let go of the lies of Satan.

Not only do we take captive the thoughts of God in our mind, but also the *words* we confess from those meditations. The words of the mouth hold the power of life or death (Prov. 18:21) ~ they either create light or bring darkness. Words of life enhance life, but they have to be synergized with the *breath* of God. As a mind focused on God's thoughts becomes united with the Holy Spirit, the force of faith goes to work.

What you set your thoughts on is what you build your life upon. What you build your life upon is the throne you establish. A throne can only house one person. Serving God is not truly servitude if you also want to be seated on that throne. If you have really given the Lordship of your life over to Jesus, and have bent your mind towards His Word through the gift of redemption, your mind will be built upon that perception.

You will also perceive others with a new mind that they too have the potential of a new mind and attitude in Christ.

I've come to realize that each of our lives matter. As long as we are alive we have one hundred percent potential to repent and turn the other way. Many times I have not had the means by which my bills can be paid. But each time I determined to lift my eyes to the possibility that in God's possibility I will not only be able to settle my bills, but also those of *others*! Expect the unexpected, for He lifts your head to see the possibilities in Him.

Psalm 3:2-3 (Amp)

"Many are saying of me, 'There is no help [no salvation] for him in God.' Selah. But You, O Lord, are a shield for me, My glory [and the honor], and the One who lifts my head"

Despite the many limitations and difficult circumstances in my life, the Holy Spirit has guided me to allowing my mind to become uncapped and unlimited to God's limitless ability. Nothing will withhold or deter me from entering into those priceless promises He has ordained for me personally, for I keep His Word and my personal prophesies in my consciousness daily. The only freedom I allow myself is in this limitless mindset of the Lord.

Whenever I feel anxiety, cares or worries, I contend for my freedom in the Lord, for the Spirit of the Lord lives within and where the Spirit of the Lord is there is liberty (2 Cor. 3:17). I invite you to determine with me to live in partnership with the Spirit in the endless possibilities in God.

THE PEACE OF FAITH

The rest, or peace, of God is our faith in the Word of God. The Holy Spirit takes us to the promises through the cleansing of our minds through the Word. This "washing" is for both our conscience and our sin.

After Jesus bought our purity and freedom, Heb. 1:3 says, *"He sat down at the right hand of the Majesty on high".* The Amplified explains that this action revealed His completed work and His Divine authority. Our understanding is therefore to stand in that victory and power with Him. Ephesians 2 reveals that we are, *"seated with Him in heavenly places".* Being seated is a picture of peace, and is portraying our shared kingly anointing and authority. A servant standing at the side of the king is attentive, yet shares in the privileges of the king. A king is seated on a throne as a symbol of authority while he is establishing the privilege of rest and peace ~ which he shares with those in his authority.

In the same way, our natural minds are attentive but our minds in Christ are attentive to act in God's sovereignty.

Jesus' last breath on earth was the declaration, *"it is finished!"* (John 19:30). Being *"in Christ"* is a perfectly, complete state of being ~ it breaks any limitation anybody has ever placed on the human mind, and breaks us through to the heavenlies where we share Christ's victory in the Spirit realm. Although we are His humble servants, He invites us as well to share His seat of authority by faith.

Our spiritual position in Christ never changes, but our soul or mind is fickle and inadequate. It is therefore not our *behavior* that needs adjusting, but our *minds* that need renewal and training. It needs conforming to this higher plane of authority ~ a heavenly way of thinking.

Our minds need to know and accept by faith our identity in Christ and what position we hold as believers. The Scripture states we not only have access to heaven at Christ's return but we are seated *with* Him right *now* in the heavenlies *"at the right hand of the Father"* (Heb. 10:12). The right hand speaks of rulership ~ our position in the Lord provides us the upper hand! We are positioned to overcome and rule on earth both in the now *and* in the future at His return.

As new creatures in Christ (2 Cor. 5:17), we are not only created for His glory within our renewed identity, but His renewed thinking enables us to

effectively *steward* the amazing authority granted to us. In essence, we were **granted a heavenly identity to enforce His earthly authority by faith!**

This authority is therefore not *of* this world but *for* this world ~ to extend the heavenly kingdom on earth that Jesus modeled during His thirty-three years of life. Studying His life we learn about the keys of the kingdom ~ the practical ways to unlock the limitations we have placed on our natural thinking. The mind of Christ will always extend longer, believe greater, see further, and will always oppose darkness. His thoughts will bring us to heavenly thinking with great authority on the earth.

RESURRECTION AUTHORITY

When Jesus breathed His last breath, He declared, *"It is finished"*, and so His earthly assignment was done. But spiritually Christ's work of reuniting us with the Father was not fully established at this point. His glory was both revealed in His covenant accomplishment *and* by granting the full and restored spiritual authority at His resurrection.

In order to understand your authority in Christ, your spirit needs *awakening.* In John

20:22 we see Jesus' first act of establishing ~ His *breathing* or blowing the Holy Spirit upon them. Jesus did this to inaugurate the birth of a new spiritual being ~ the *"second Adam"*.

When God breathed life into the nostrils of Adam (Gen. 2:7); He was literally teaching Adam *how* to breathe and how to *have* life. But when Jesus breathed into us again, we became a *"life-giving spirit"*. He was teaching us how to *give* life (1 Cor. 15:45). When we live through the life of Christ, we are enforcing His true life-giving authority in the earth. The kingdom is spiritually within, manifesting physically.

A recent testimony illustrates the resurrection power of the Lord active in our meetings. A man's ex-wife called to report that he had died. There was no pulse and His heart had stopped.

I sensed in the Spirit that he would come back to life. I agreed with my brother Timothy Snodgrass who was with me at the time. Shortly thereafter we received the amazing news that he had miraculously come back to life! This man now lives by the power of God!

CREO

CHAPTER 7
BREAKTHROUGH MIND

೦ঙ৪০

Receiving Christ is also receiving His mind, intelligence, genius or mind capacity. This miracle is not fathomable by the limited human mind but by the aid of the genius indwelling Holy Spirit. Although His mind is incomprehensible, one thousand steps ahead of the most genius natural mind of man, our partnership with Him brings us into a realm we ourselves do not comprehend.

That is why we communicate and operate with the Lord by faith. This is breakthrough thinking ~ a way of thinking that has broken through into the heavenlies.

GENIUS MINDS

Solomon was supernaturally equipped when God visited him.

1 Kings 3:10-14

"The speech pleased the Lord, that Solomon had asked this thing. Then God said to him: 'Because you have asked this thing, and have not asked long life for yourself, nor have asked riches for yourself, nor have asked the life of your enemies, but have asked for yourself understanding to discern justice, behold, I have done according to your words; see, I have given you a wise and understanding heart, so that there has not been anyone like you before you, nor shall any like you arise after you. And I have also given you what you have not asked: both riches and honour, so that there shall not be anyone like you among the kings all your days. So if you walk in My ways, to keep My statutes and My commandments, as your father David walked, then I will lengthen your days.'"

Through the impartation of wisdom and understanding Solomon was able to build a kingdom like no other.

Likewise, Peter and John were given bold speech that astounded the Sanhedrin (Acts 4:13). Christ's mind transforms us today from being mediocre to becoming dependently genius.

Israel was transitioning from a mentality of slavery to rulership when they encountered the greatest natural limitation at the Red Sea. The miracle of that huge body of water parting was a lesson in transitioning their thinking.

Where their possibilities ended, God's possibilities started.

With the looming threat of the charging Egyptians, their cries to the Lord were desperate but some of them were full of faith in God to come through on their behalf. I imagine they thought the miracle would happen in the form of God sweeping them up in a cloud and planting them safely on the other side. But the Lord wanted them to develop a *breakthrough* mindset ~ an attitude of nothing-can-stop-us and limitless-obedience to the Lord Almighty.

The power of the Lord within has great advancing qualities. It levels the mountains and raises the valleys in our physical and spiritual environments.

Isaiah 40:4 (AMP)

"Every valley shall be raised,
And every mountain and hill be made low;
And let the rough ground become a plain,
And the rugged places a broad valley"

GROUNDBREAKING MINDS

Just like engineering technology has brought much development to modern living and property development, spiritually we advance as well. Our faith "bulldozes" through hard ground and builds mansions on mountains never excavated before. Today you have the capacity to build where previously there was no possibility of this.

Let us therefore grow in expectation, open and expand our minds to greater possibilities ~ to the greater things the Lord has purposed for us in these times. He has prepared pleasant places for us.

The Israelites were not only trained in advanced thinking, but to *advancing* thinking in their transition from slavery to occupying Canaan. I believe the time span for advancement is getting shorter and shorter as the generations progress quicker and more effectively in the Lord. May the forty-year mind renewal happen to us in a concentrated time in the Spirit.

If you stay on course with the Lord things will advance. Your life can only develop and grow. Thinking the Word and never undermining or underestimating God's thoughts will allow you to envision the picture He will paint with your life. Without His Word insanity and failure is imminent, so keep this vision of His Word before you. The Word is a powerful weapon ~ a double-edged Sword able to cut away and destroy that part of your destructive and emotional thinking. He is able to complete what He's started in you and is able to keep you holy and separated until His return. Agree with the word of the Lord in this Psalm. Confess this over your life:

Psalm 16:6 (MSG)

"My choice is You, GOD, first and only.
And now I find I'm Your choice!

114

You set me up with a house and yard.
And then You made me Your heir!"

LIKE JESUS

Like the great minds of old, you have the illuminated mind of Christ to unite with God, to submit to Him and dispel the works and strategies of the enemy. Do not be deceived to think that only good works and deeds, without a first-hand knowledge of Christ, makes us any different than an unbeliever who by only their *conscience* is kind and generous.

Jesus started this genuine, overcoming abundant life residing in our spirit-man by His covenant on the cross. He paid for us to have a new attitude, a new spirit and a new way of thinking. The Holy Spirit is our residing companion who is always willing and more than able to help us govern our minds and overcome the temptations of the carnal nature to be one with Him.

Many believers, however, feel stuck in the harsh realities of life and circumstances. This is not your true reality. The truth is, you are above all that! Your heavenly identity and your position next to Jesus is the real you! The Holy Spirit is ready to reveal to your personally, the reality of you seated in heavenly places with Him.

Before we were reunited with the Holy Spirit our minds were independent and unenlightened.

Considering the state of our world today, we are remorsefully reminded of what man's darkened mind has achieved over thousands of years. Dependent, overcoming thinking with Christ is what you were created for. Independent thinking is part of your old life. You have stepped out of being dysfunctional and into maturity! Your renewal not only covers your intellect, but your emotions and your will as well!

This place of overcoming in your mind is therefore not dependent on anything happening to you or around you. Economy, traumas, death, disease, or anxieties have no hold on your place in the heavenlies. It is therefore your responsibility to daily delve deeper into God's Presence and His Word ~ to walk within the extraordinary advantages of the mind of Christ. You were made to overcome through a higher vantage point in this life!

Your mind in Christ was created first of all for you but also for others. You are the steward of it to develop, to mature and hold the endless resources of the heavens. We were granted this breakthrough blessing to build a legacy of Godly leadership, overcoming character and extraordinary wisdom. If the minds of Solomon and Daniel, who only had the Spirit *upon* them, enforced great respect and power in the presence of ungodly Babylonian and Egyptian leaders ~ think of the unlimited influence believers can have today!

We are breakthrough thinkers who have the Spirit of Christ *within* us!

The following points of manifest authority are quite extensive, but your heart and mind need to grasp it by the Holy Spirit. Do not be deceived that the manifestations were only meant for accounts in Scripture. God united you to Him in the Spirit for physical empowerment!

See yourself making disciples, baptizing, and teaching the Word (Matt. 28:16-20). Also contemplate the signs that are to follow your faith: the casting out of demons, speaking in tongues, and not being harmed by poisonous snakebites (Mark 16:14-18). If you don't visualize and expect opportunities, it is most unlikely you will not have the faith and courage to activate them!

THE MIND OF THE SHEPHERD

We are becoming like Jesus, who is the Good Shepherd. Also included in your authority arsenal is love and forgiveness: *"If you forgive the sins of anyone they are forgiven [because of their faith]; if you retain the sins of anyone they are retained [and remain unforgiven because of their unbelief"* (John 20:23- Amp). This verse says you are not only to preach the way of salvation, but also warn those who reject the gospel through hard hearts and unbelief.

117

As the Father sent Jesus, He also sends you (John 20:21). You are unified with heaven to respond in love to the Lord now that He has filled you with His Spirit. Just as Jesus asked Simon Peter to prove his love for Him, so the Lord has granted you more than enough, to not only feed your mind, but to feed His lambs and to tend and feed His sheep.

John 21:15-19 (Message)

"After breakfast, Jesus said to Simon Peter, 'Simon, son of John, do you love me more than these?'

'Yes, Master, you know I love You.'

Jesus said, 'Feed My lambs.'

He then asked a second time, 'Simon, son of John, do you love Me?'

'Yes, Master, You know I love You.'

Jesus said, 'Shepherd My sheep.'

Then He said it a third time: 'Simon, son of John, do you love Me?'

Peter was upset that He asked for the third time, 'Do you love Me?' so he answered, 'Master, You know everything there is to know. You've got to know that I love You.'

Jesus said, 'Feed My sheep. I'm telling you the very truth now: When you were young you dressed yourself and went wherever you wished, but when you get old you'll have to stretch out your hands while someone else dresses you and takes you where you don't want to go.'

He said this to hint at the kind of death by which Peter would glorify God. And then He commanded, 'Follow Me.'"

Why could Cain not accept the mind of God when his sacrifice was not accepted? (Genesis 1:4-8). He did not understand that a true sacrifice God accepts is associated with the condition of the heart. If the heart is filled with love ~ the sacrifice (work) is accepted by Him. It is vital therefore that we have a heart and mind of love to break ground in the natural realm

VALUING THE GOSPEL

Knowing that we prove our love for the Lord by discipling others, the sharing of the Gospel of Christ should have the highest regard in our thinking. It is therefore wise to give it the commitment and honor it is due. It holds the very favorable thoughts and solutions of God towards the challenges and vices of humankind. The Gospel is the power of God that saves us and has stood strong and faithful like an unmovable lighthouse through the storms and challenges of time.

Romans 1:16 (AMP)

"I am not ashamed of the gospel, for it is the power of God for salvation [from His wrath and punishment] to everyone who believes [in Christ as Savior], to the Jew first and also to the Greek"

Amidst human philosophies, humanism, political and educational knowledge, and technological developments, the Gospel of Christ has stood steady through every test and conquered every challenge history has thrown at it.

Let us consider with renewed vigor, the tremendous value of the Word of God. Throughout the history of time, men, women and children have given their lives to stand for the Gospel ~ and many have suffered and endured dangers, trials, and persecution to defend and continue the availability of the Word of God to us today. Let us not grow casual about the priceless treasure of the Bible that has remained available to our children. May a continued urgency be upheld to preach the gospel today in all the corners of the world, and not just on the mission-fields. The Gospel is our very life ~ our stewardship in presenting its truth to young and old *is* a matter of life and death.

Many children raised in Christian or missionary homes tend to underestimate the significance and power of what their parents or forefathers had to sacrifice or forfeit to enable them to pass the Gospel onto the next generation. The result is in most other cases a religious mindset about the Bible and a cold attitude about faith. That is why it is vital that we do not stop at only reading Bible Stories, attending church or youth programs. Young people need to be given practical, experiential opportunities to build their own testimonies as soon as possible in their lives.

The most effective way of getting the Gospel to a certain age group is not just from adults, but inviting the most influential group to minister the authentic truth of God's Word. For example, teens are mostly impacted by on-fire, enthusiastic twenty-something year olds. The practical demonstration of the work of the Spirit must also be pursued in these stages of maturity.

The essence and truth of the Gospel is a personal and vital understanding to be shared so that the power of the Gospel will be made real to each person.

1 Corinthians 4:20 (Amp)

"For the kingdom of God is not based on talk but on power"

Imagine the effect one generation will have on the next. When parents manage to serve their children with the authentic power of the Gospel? The great advantage of eternal life and spiritual maturity has many times been gained at the cost of a family's financial sacrifice. Ultimately, these children have gained a priceless heritage through consistent mentoring and learned stewardship, including many hours of parents praying for their children. The following Scripture reveals how heaven values this great commitment.

Daniel 12:3 (Amp)

"Those who are [spiritually] wise will shine brightly like the brightness of the expanse of heaven, and those who lead many to righteousness, [will shine] like the stars forever and ever"

It is of utmost importance that we place a renewed value on the privilege and honor of the Gospel of Christ while we have the time to do so. Too many people have become familiar with the Bible being so available, and thereby have underestimated its significance and power.

Those of you who have influence in businesses, schools, and governments have a great opportunity to communicate the importance and priceless value of the truth of the Gospel ~ and how much we need it in today's business and life! The more you do this, the more people will recognize the value of it and the more funds will be made available to further the Gospel through the vast forms of communication available today.

You have freely been given the grace of rebirth in Christ. Therefore I declare that you have many opportunities lying ahead to be giving your gifts freely for the furtherance of the Gospel. I pray that greatly effective forms of communication, like television broadcasting and printing of books, will be handled with so much wisdom and care that it will not cause God's house of prayer to seem like a house of merchandise

Matt. 21:13 (Message)

"Jesus went straight to the Temple and threw out everyone who had set up shop, buying and selling. He kicked over the tables of loan sharks and the stalls of dove merchants. He quoted this text: 'My house was designated a house of prayer; you have made it a hangout for thieves.'

Now there was room for the blind and crippled to get in. They came to Jesus and he healed them"

I declare there is blessing upon every selfless sacrifice you have made for Him ~ whether you have given time, talents, or treasures ~ however small or great. He will amazingly multiply even the smallest efforts you have made for the Gospel unto His glory. Your generosity, hospitality, and giving nature (granted to you by the applied mind of Christ) can only increase.

May your generous spirit, bringing true worship to the Lord, leave room for those who are truly seeking the Lord for healing and deliverance. You are blessed to be a blessing!

In a church in Rialto, one man had a paralyzed arm for many years. After the Word and prayer, he received life back in his arm and was able to use it without any problems. It was truly miraculous!

Many other people at this meeting were healed of neck and back issues ~ and were also healed of cancer!

We are walking with Jesus in the supernatural power of His love. We have entered into the realm of the heavens. We will walk in breakthrough thinking.

જી**૪**

CHAPTER 8

PARTNERING WITH GOD

ⵊⵊ

John 4:10

"But whoever drinks of the water that I shall give him will never thirst. But the water that I shall give him will become in him a fountain of water springing up into everlasting life"

YOU ARE INSEPARABLE

It is known that water is the primarily nourishment needed by the body, and especially the brain, in order for the whole body to function optimally. Just like our bodies need seventy-five percent water, our partnership with God's nourishment is vital for life. The mind of Christ needs hydration and cleansing.

Just like our bodies need daily care of washing and cleansing, the living waters of His person hydrate and cleanse our spirits. As water is vital, so the mind of Christ keeps us optimal.

Not only does His living water nourish us but we are also "cleansed by the washing of the water of the word". This is such a beautiful illustration of how God nurtures and intimately cares for His own. Husbands are likened to this leadership of God when they minister to their spouses by *"washing"* them with the word in order to present them holy unto the Lord.

Ephesians 5:25-27.

"Husbands, love your wives, just as Christ also loved the church and gave Himself for her, that He might sanctify and cleanse her with the washing of water by the word, that He might present her to Himself a glorious church, not having spot or wrinkle or any such thing, but that she should be holy and without blemish"

I believe the ministry of the cleansing Word of God is not limited to the preference of the gender delivering it. Otherwise women would not be allowed to read the Bible for themselves. Since we are all called as priests and kings, anyone, regardless of gender, has the authority to minister the word of God to themselves and to others.

Since you are inseparable by the union of the Holy Spirit, God has already provided everything for you. Not only is He busy preparing a place for you in heaven, but He has provided certain things on earth for your full nourishment and nurturing right now!

This concept of the Lord's presence being like water and rain comes from the ancient manuscripts, and can be noted throughout Scriptures. I highlight from Psalm 46:4-7 to reveal that God Himself is like a nourishing river to each person.

Psalm 46:4-7 (NKJV)

"There is a river whose streams shall make glad the city of God, the holy place of the tabernacle of the Most High. God is in the midst of her, she shall not be moved; God shall help her, just at the break of dawn. The nations raged, the kingdoms were moved; He uttered His voice, the earth melted. The Lord of hosts is with us; the God of Jacob is our refuge. Selah"

Here we see that this central reservoir of His presence is even available to all the God-fearing nations of the world. What more reasons do we need to live life celebrating in this river of joy, which cascades from His throne? Do we tap into this flow of life with continuous thanksgiving, worship and praise? Are we testimonies of no longer being subject to the effects of a decaying word?

As we are heading for that "pure river of water of life" (Rev. 22:1) in the eternal city, we live sustained by that very water each day, right now. We are now the mobile, living, holy tabernacle and the city of God where He dwells.

This position in Christ means we were eternally provided for, lacking nothing, nor ever spiritually dehydrated or malnourished! How great and awesome is our God who fulfills all our needs. He is truly the perfect Provider, the faithful Father. You are inseparable!

PARTNERING WITH OTHERS

The "rivers of living water" coming from the presence of God is evident, in that our connection with God is not only for *our* benefit but also for the vital sustenance of *others.*

Much of our most severe past failures have been relationally based through inadequate mindsets. This has much to do with our human nature wanting to operate by independent thoughts ~ thinking and operating apart from God. When you contemplate your life, you might be living with the regret of missed opportunities. You wished you had completed your education, made different career choices, or even married someone else. Some of us celebrate great decisions and others live with poor decisions. But most people, even the best of them, live with the regret of not partnering with God and with those who He has ordained to walk with.

I believe it is God's design for each person to live *without* regrets, even without sin, by becoming totally dependent upon His thoughts and mind. Even though He emits pure holiness, He knows our humanity completely (Heb. 4:15).

You can avoid living with regret by following the intuitions God has made available to your mind. He can enlighten your thinking and empower you to be guided through life's challenges. This doesn't mean God cannot also *direct* you to the right relationship by using common sense or by acquiring godly counsel to make informed decisions. It's all about you standing confident in your identity in Him through your personal partnership with Him.

God determined that our union in Him would enable us to be relationally successful, yet not degenerate towards humanism. In our partnership with others it is important to note the "unequal yoke" that the mindset of the world brings.

2 Corinthians 6:14)

"Do not be unequally yoked together with unbelievers. For what fellowship has righteousness with lawlessness? And what communion has light with darkness?"

We are daily dealing with a great onslaught by the mindset of humanism. This evil (dark), lawless, deceitful spirit is deeply Anti-Christ and can be found in all spheres of society. It appears very pleasant, enticing and good, but it has a destructive core that cannot survive by care of itself. We study it in many kinds of symbolism laid out in the book of

Revelation (that is a study for another day). Perhaps, the Dictionary defines humanism best:

"A system of thought that is based on the values, characteristics, and behavior that are believed to be best in human beings, rather than on any supernatural authority."

We are in opposition to the spirit of humanism ~ since we are connected to God in spirit, soul and body ~ and are partnered with God's highest values of love. Our character is an imitation of the life and character of Jesus Christ the Son of God. Our behavior flows from the authority of His word. We also do not base our faith upon personal preferences that are harmful to others. Unbelievers believe in their own preferences about gender, abortion, drugs, abnormal ways of dressing, and so on. Humanism attempts to solve current world problems but lacks the long-term wisdom to uphold the eternal values of the Creator.

Since believing disciples build *with* God on an unshakeable kingdom, we do not build upon our personal preferences but on unreserved obedience. As a result, we are not people pleasing but primarily God-pleasing! That means that misunderstanding, persecution, abandonment, rejection and excommunication become part of the package of faith. This should not deter the believer or get them to relent to the yoke with the world, but be yoked closer into friendship with Jesus, whose "yoke is easy and whose burden is light."

Matthew 11:28-30 (NKJV)

"Come to Me, all you who labour and are heavy laden, and I will give you rest. Take My yoke upon you and learn from Me, for I am gentle and lowly in heart, and you will find rest for your souls. For My yoke is easy and My burden is light"

Partnerships that are not *of* God or *in* God will be predominantly laborsome and heavy. They will not be gentle and humble. You will always need to prove yourself and you still find no rest for your soul. Does this sound familiar to you? I hope not!

Living in a God-given partnership is a light, pleasant yoke that does not burden you with the expectations and preferences of humanism or vainly trying to be someone else. His thoughts are much higher than any human being or human-designed system, and that is the mind you follow and submit to. We do not come under a dictatorship's influence and control ~ but a loving, faith-filled absolute as we walk in obedience to God. The mind (word) of Christ is unequivocal – it is not capable of being viewed as partial or relative. By absolute proof the word of the Lord has been refined "seven times" for it to be a mindset that is totally dependable. His word is the base upon which we build our relationships and partnerships.

Psalm 12:6

"The words of the LORD are pure words, like silver tried in a furnace of earth, purified seven times"

The mind of Christ is available and accessible to every believer, since it has primarily been granted by His blood for our complete restoration. That means that whatever bondage you were in (whether it be any kind of "isms") when you found Christ, your "shame" became a means of testifying to your freedom.

Your continued commitment to beholding your splendid identity as you seek the face of God will bring you to a partnership with Him and with others. You willingly partner with His ways of thinking since He is your Superior. It *is* possible to live a life devoid of regrets!

MYSTERY OF HOLY SPIRIT SYNERGY

Mysteries can be complicated, but with the mind of Christ every heavenly mystery is unraveled to us by the Holy Spirit (Ephesians 3:5). That is why we are wasting our time by over-thinking and strategizing without the help of the Spirit. He is the One who partners you with heaven. Many times we do not know what the Spirit is going to do. The feeling of "being out of control" should really be combated by an acceptance that God holds the steering wheel and we are merely passengers in His plan ~ yet we are in synergy with His mind.

Many times He only requires us to take the next step by faith, heed to the last prophetic word, and not know the whole plan.

Christ has taken the pressure off ~ He has invited us into stress-free anxiety-free living for His glory. We do not know how He enlarges our hearts in the process, but we just know that He is able to accomplish what only He is able to do.

Apostle Paul regarded the process of mind-renewal as a mystery. You need not be confused, concerned, or anxious about the process God is conducting in you once you have committed to having your thoughts renewed. By faith you only need to cooperate with His supernatural special under-cover assignment in your very heart, working the stealth-warfare against the enemy's evil assignments. It is, after all, His work and not yours that has already won the victory. You are the happy enforcer who gets to share in His glory!

Welcome the inexplicable transformation that is occurring, despite criticisms and condemnations trying to distract you from keeping your eyes on Jesus! You are just to receive it as a part of the work of Christ on the cross for you personally. All you have to do is daily cooperate with His glorious under-cover strategies while you are in joyful praise, prayer and worship!

Consider how the jail doors were supernaturally opened while Paul and Silas were worshiping and praising the Lord (Acts 16:16-34). It was a total mystery how they could sing amidst the pain of being pummeled and scourged, and how they got out of being executed for opposing the divination-spirit.

But the power of God preserved them in their simple submission and trust in the Lord. God is truly building "baffling grit" in each of us!

Paul wrote an encouragement to the Colossians concerning this mysterious process, as it seems that this was his main focus and assignment in bringing believers to maturity:

Colossians 1:26-29 (MSG)

"This mystery has been kept in the dark for a long time, but now it's out in the open. God wanted everyone, not just Jews, to know this rich and glorious secret inside and out, regardless of their background, regardless of their religious standing. The mystery in a nutshell is just this: Christ is in you, so therefore you can look forward to sharing in God's glory. It's that simple. That is the substance of our Message. We preach Christ, warning people not to add to the Message. We teach in a spirit of profound common sense so that we can bring each person to maturity. To be mature is to be basic. Christ! No more, no less. That's what I'm working so hard at day after day, year after year; doing my best with the energy God so generously gives me"

THE PRODUCE OF PARTNERSHIP

Partnering with God is not done with your mind, but with your heart partnering with God's heart and mind. The cross of Christ is that bridge that brings heaven to your mind.

Coming to the understanding of the message of the cross, and how God created us in His image as spiritual faith-filled beings, is the wisest thing you can ever do! This will bring an end to anything that has corrupted your way of thinking and living.

When you are thinking and acting like God, you are not thinking from your head (soul or intelligence), but you're thinking from the heart or from your spirit man. Insisting on understanding God in your own mind will inevitably produce a limited view of Him, which produces religion and destruction.

Luke 6:45 (Amp)

"The [intrinsically] good man produces what is good and honorable and moral out of the good treasure [stored] in his heart; and the [intrinsically] evil man produces what is wicked and depraved out of the evil [in his heart]; for his mouth speaks from the overflow of his heart."

1 Corinthians 2:16 (Amp)

"For who has known the mind and purposes of the Lord, so as to instruct Him? But we have the mind of Christ [to be guided by His thoughts and purposes]"

135

In much of our modern culture the power of the natural or carnal mind is much too highly esteemed. Since we have been given the mind of Christ we are spiritually connected to heaven. In James 3:15, the Word of God gives us the answer to this:

"This [superficial] wisdom is not that which comes down from above, but is earthly (secular), natural (unspiritual), even demonic"

See how the "secular" and the "unspiritual" has influenced our thinking. Meditating upon and obedience to, the words of Christ have miraculous ways of healing us. Jesus guarantees His way of thinking, which is heavenly and spiritual, is like building upon a rock instead of the sandy strongholds of the world.

The most intelligent and spiritual person of his day, a priest named Nicodemus, came to Jesus at nighttime to seek answers. Jesus realized an even greater need in him, coming right to the point by explaining the limitations of his mind to spiritual things.

John 3:7-8 (Amp):

"Do not be surprised that I have told you, 'You must be born again [reborn from above—spiritually transformed, renewed, sanctified].' The wind blows where it wishes and you hear its sound, but you do not know where it is coming from and where it is going; so it is with everyone who is born of the Spirit"

Once you've received the miracle of spiritual rebirth, you have been restored to your true self, which is being primarily spirit. That doesn't mean you are now living mindlessly, but shifting your focus on Jesus, the True Vine; and the Father who is the Vinedresser (John 15).

You have been transferred from self-dependence, or independence, to your dependence upon God. You trade your sense of trust in anything mortal to a total, abandoned faith-filled trust in God who is immortal. Jesus said when you loose these trust you trade the temporal for the eternal.

Matthew 10:39 (Amp)

"Whoever finds his life [in this world] will [eventually] lose it [through death], and whoever loses his life [in this world] for My sake will find it [that is, life with Me for all eternity]"

You no longer tap from your source of carnal thinking by depending on your own intellect, emotions or will, but you regard yourself engrafted or rooted in the Spirit of God. This is what Jesus' life, death and resurrection accomplished for us! It produced a partnership of our inheritance. We did not deserve it: we only have to receive it.

As mentioned before, being rooted in the Lord means your essence, or DNA, is made up of one thing and that is love ~ for that one little word defines all His glory. You have been translated to operate from the heart, and *then* from the head. From birth to death, to resurrection and rulership, Jesus portrayed and embodied the love of the Father. Agree with the Apostle Paul and be encouraged to be *"rooted and grounded in love"* (Ephesians 3:17), for He is love. Our source of strength and power produces one thing and that is the love of God.

If there has ever been a lack in fruitfulness, the disconnection happened when love was forsaken.

Paul emphasized this connectedness in the analogy of a child acting and wanting to be like his or her dad. That pure love, that admiration and trust, is the emphasis here. He directed the churches in Ephesus, Thessalonica and Corinthia to be *"imitators of God"*. If we, like adoring children, are to be imitators of God, let us look at the ways of the Lord as portrayed in Scripture. There are a few analogies from nature that we can look at to better understand what God is accomplishing in us.

THE WIND OF CHANGE

Jesus told Nicodemus that the Holy Spirit is *"like the wind"*. He explained the three attributes of the Holy Spirit that are like the wind: He can be heard, He cannot be seen, and He comes and goes as He pleases. We can only see the *effect* the wind has on the environment, and so we can only stand in praise and wonder at what He accomplished in and through us.

That is why a lifestyle of thanksgiving, praise and worship is the imitation of the wind-like attribute He is forming within us.

Let us also not limit the Holy Spirit in meetings to only singing hymns or songs, but allow Him to pray, groan, weep, and even violently sound through our lives.

As we allow our minds to be renewed He will produce the pure sound of worship that the enemy fears so much. Consider why God used the pure sound of the praises of the tribe of Judah to go before the army to confuse the enemy and win the victory (1 Chronicles 20).

Consider too the account of Paul and Silas being imprisoned in jail, and how they were miraculously freed from their bonds through the act of worship (Acts 16:24-26). Their praises were a means of partnering with God, and He replied in the form of an earthquake that put the jailers in a trance and freed them from their bonds. It is known that earthquakes are focused at depths well out of the reach of weather, and the forces that cause earthquakes are much larger than the weather's forces! This is the extent and the trouble God will take to partner with His children.

If we are imitating the Holy Spirit, that doesn't necessarily mean that it licenses us to "improvise" as we please. Some Christians are not content with the unpredictable "sailboat lifestyle" of being dependent on the winds of the Spirit. They resist the adventure of faith by keeping an engine on their vessels of life, when they signed up to work on a sailboat! They have traded a man-made, lifeless engine for the glorious sails that ride the winds of change. We have signed up to be those fishermen on His boat and to do His bidding, as *the Captain pleases.*

If you are one with Him, it sets you free like those billowing sails. It unfetters you to bend and to go as far and long as He pleases, to the places that lead to adventure and fulfillment. Blessed are the flexible! If Christ came not to please Himself (Philippians 2:7), but the Father, then have we truly submitted to the Holy Spirit regenerative process when we are willfully pleasing ourselves (or even others) above the Father?

It is no wonder that the manner in which His Spirit was sent on the day of Pentecost (Acts 2), was a sound "rushing" and "violent". This sounds like passionate, fierce and intense love as we look again at the Amplified account in verses 1 to 4:

> *"When the day of Pentecost had come, they were all together in one place, and suddenly a sound came from heaven like a rushing violent wind, and it filled the whole house where they were sitting. There appeared to them tongues resembling fire, which were being distributed [among them], and they rested on each one of them [as each person received the Holy Spirit]. And they were all filled [that is, diffused throughout their being] with the Holy Spirit*

140

and began to speak in other tongues (different languages), as the Spirit was giving them the ability to speak out [clearly and appropriately]."

Through your consistent faith-filled attitude of thanksgiving, praise, and worship, you govern all thoughts, decisions and motives from your spiritual intuition and discernment.

Your primary source of thinking is by means of God's thoughts and not with your head (or brain). You are thinking from your core, your heart, and flowing with the glorious and passionate wind of His breath. That doesn't mean you will be living mindlessly, but simply partnering with God as a lifestyle. You are partnering with God Himself, which includes partaking of all His gifts and resources.

PARTNERSHIP GROWTH

A partnership has to grow or it loses connectedness. The opposite of this love-core develops a stronghold of prideful thinking and can even develop an enmity of staying connected to God. The same thing happens in marriage.

Pride is the most combative battle in the mind, a deception that wants to figure out all the variables, to depend on opinions and philosophies without authentic relationship. Deception is the result ~ even like a stronghold which believes that the priority of relationship

141

and good communication is unspiritual and a waste of time.

The truth of effective partnerships and remaining connected to the Holy Spirit never prohibits the development of the mind of Christ in relationships.

In truth, it is the easiest and most fun-filled thing to stay in favor with God and with man but religious, demonically inspired thinking has caused people to think otherwise. Luke 2:52 (Amp) says:

> *"And Jesus kept increasing in wisdom and in stature, and in favor with God and men"*

Jesus modeled partnership when calling and living with His disciples. He introduced Himself by calling each one by their name ~ sometimes using the gift of discernment to not only know their birth names but their spiritual, prophetic names. May we connect to the right God-ordained partnerships by the Spirit.

Trust allows a partnership to grow. When Jesus walked with His disciples His preference for simple, yet intimate and meaningful, *friendship* has always invited all those in proximity to come really close to His heart (Matthew 28:11). So many spiritual leaders (or those just focusing on discipling others) get distracted by the intense responsibilities of leadership. They land up not really engaging people's hearts in the process and so forfeiting their trust. Yet there is also a dual responsibility of both leaders and those being discipled.

Many Christians have accepted the shelter of the Father's house, even dancing with the Father, but they have never accepted the opportunity to "*sit* on His lap" like a confident son or daughter.

This is the desire of the Father for each believer ~ that they come close enough to find His heart, His mind, His voice and His desire; to enjoy a deep and meaningful daily touch.

Scripture teaches that depending on our unrenewed, orphaned mind in connecting with God is foolishness. This was expounded to the Corinthians by the Apostle Paul in the first chapter and verse 25 of the Amplified version:

> "[This is] **because the foolishness of God** [is not foolishness at all and] **is wiser than men** [far beyond human comprehension], **and the weakness of God is stronger than men** [far beyond the limits of human effort]."

Resolve today to stay active in discerning your own heart by remaining in touch with the heart and mind of God. Remain in the flow of His Holy Spirit without any hindrances caused by unbelief.

In my ministry my partnership with God is the most essential priority. Each and every time I minister or bring forth a sermon, my connection with Him enables me to accomplish what I start out to do. For me, each time I step onto a ministry platform, whether public or private, my dependence is one hundred percent upon Him. This might sound strange to you, but as much as I depend upon Him, He also depends on me one hundred percent! We have a dual partnership of trust with His most precious bride. He depends on me to act upon that which He reveals to me.

May your faith-filled partnership with the Lord bring you to a relationship of one hundred percent trust by the Holy Spirit. As He reveals His heart to you about the ministry opportunities He has opened to you, may you faithfully act upon them responsibly and in the fear of the Lord.

THE FAITH OF PARTNERSHIP

Many fall into the error of independence through unbelief, and think that since He is invisible He is silently uninvolved! Push this unbelief far away from your thinking! He is a person, He has incredible thoughts, a passionate heart, emotion, and intention. Though He has a mind of His own, He still desires to participate in your personal walk with Him. He wants to advise and counsel you, as He knows your independent humanity is insufficient.

Allow Him to by faith "take over" all the time, and then obey Him by taking charge and stewarding that which He entrusts you with. Don't allow anybody or anything to interfere or distract you from that which He has placed in *your* personal responsibility. As a spiritual leader you also have the ability to discern the "control freakishness," a need to stay busy or to perform that can easily beset. This is due to fear crouching at the door of faith. Meanwhile, the Holy Spirit is providing that perfect, peaceful balance and wisdom that allows you to walk within the authority of your inheritance as a covenant son of God.

Being in partnership with God means He has the *main* part in the joint ventures He sets up. He is like the Executive Director. You do not arrange something without His direction, and then include Him as a "spare part". You maintain the principle of allowing Him to remain involved in *everything* since He always has time for you.

That means planning your time management, which includes meeting with Him before decisions are made. Just like business partners plan their meeting strategies, so we make place for God's sovereignty.

It doesn't mean you're a "puppet on a string", for He honors your individuality and humanity. When you don't understand what He is requesting or leading you into, He still values your opinion. But He disregards things that do not contribute to your partnership, like complaining or being negative.

It is up to *you* to *search out the matter* when He speaks to you. He wants to download the mind of Christ to you in the event. If you do not understand, just ask Him about it in prayer.

Proverbs 25:2 (NKJV)

"It is the glory of God to conceal a matter, but the glory of kings is to search out a matter"

How awesome is our unequaled God, who takes the time to partner with His creation! What a great adventure we are engaged in to bring restoration to the corruption that humanity has brought to His design. Let us draw close and quickly draw close today!

James 4:8 (NKJV)

"Draw near to God and He will draw near to you"

ೞ

CHAPTER 9
CO-OPERATING WITH GOD

☙❧

THINK FROM THE HEART

Thinking from the heart comes from the ability to *hear* by faith with the *heart*, not with physical ears. This also goes for both natural and supernatural relationships. Although the Lord speaks audibly, it is most likely He wants us to co-operate with Him by hearing His voice *intuitively* ~ through the faith of our spirit-person, the heart.

Visualize yourself practicing this daily. Heed those gentle promptings when reading His Word; going about your daily life recognizing His signs in various ways. Humbly posture yourself to learn from Him for He is always speaking. This is truly the greatest miracle as was demonstrated by the Lord speaking to Elijah in the still small voice instead of the fiery storm. Obedience to His voice is therefore your most valuable asset. It is your spiritual wealth. It is you co-operating with God.

1 Samuel 15:22 (Amp)

"Samuel said,' Has the Lord as great a delight in burnt offerings and sacrifices as in obedience to the voice of the Lord? Behold, to obey is better than sacrifice, and to heed [is better] than the fat of rams'"

HOW THE MIND AND HEART RELATE

Most people are self-focused and have a high awareness of how their bodies relate to the mind. Others are spiritually focused and have some understanding of the dimensions of the spirit and body ~ but there seems to be a general limited understanding of the heart. This is because most people don't realize that God created the heart, so in order to understand it you have to get to know Him first.

God is not swayed by our humanness, although He does not totally disregard us since the very reason He sent His son for its restoration. He primarily regards the *hearts* of humans, so we should not feel justified to neglect the study of our minds.

Jeremiah says that even though the heart is the seat of God, without the Lord our hearts are deceitful.

Jeremiah 17:9-10 (MSG)

"The heart is hopelessly dark and deceitful, a puzzle that no one can figure out. But I, God, search the heart and examine the mind. I get to the heart of the human. I get to the root of things. I treat them as they really are, not as they pretend to be"

Our hearts can only become deceitful once our motives are not rooted in the mind of Christ. Our motives come from that deep-seated, hidden subconscious place which God longs to totally occupy. If we do not make our heart God's home, there will always be a void in our emotions and a heart searching for fulfillment.

Understanding your heart is thereby, coming to understand fulfillment. Even though it is God's work bringing us to complete maturity, He loves us to have a sense of accomplishment, achievement, and performance reward that comes from co-operating with God. He placed that desire of fulfillment in our hearts. Jesus taught this principle to His disciples during the Sermon on the Mount in Matthew 5. This statement reveals that the greatest human desire of the heart is to be one with God and to be in right standing with Him ~ to co-operate with Him.

Matthew 5:6 (AMP)

"Blessed [joyful, nourished by God's goodness] are those who hunger and thirst

for righteousness [those who actively seek right standing with God], for they will be [completely] satisfied"

HOW TO CO-OPERATE WITH GOD

How do we actively seek co-operation or right standing with God? Your mind is the manager or butler of your soul (intellect, will, emotions). Your heart is the product of the stewardship of the soul. But it is also a synergy of your co-operation with the Holy Spirit to keep that space in an immaculate renewed condition ~ producing the process of a renewed mind. We call this the mind of Christ.

You have the mind of Christ but you also have possession of your own mind. Even though you might be sitting in a car, you still have to shift the gear to advance forward. To grow in maturity you need His cooperation. Only *you* can put your mind in the right direction.

Then your mind goes into gear. Depending on the condition of renewal, it is able to filter what is "taken to heart". To take something to heart is an idiom used to emphasize taking something seriously; to internalize or live according to something. The heart filters and absorbs things that lead to eventual actions of either life or death. Cooperating with God is advancing *forward* in life!

When a heart has "absorbed" the essence of God through the ranges of drawing near to Him, we draw near to His great love. His love is our reward, our destination and home. It's the event, where we come to a sense of completion, which is living in His "love-light". Our hearts are filled with what it was made to carry; yet it is free and uncontaminated.

There is no blockage, shortage, or unfulfillment. It is at total peace and rest. "Shalom" in the Hebrew sums this up so perfectly. It expands the meaning of peace to include harmony, wholeness, completeness, prosperity, welfare and tranquility; and can be used idiomatically to mean both hello and goodbye. When your heart and mind are clean, your home and life will be too!

The mind of the heart is like a motor engine in pristine condition, able to direct the body in the right direction ~the heart of God. Your heart cannot operate effectively without having the mind renewed. But if it is, the heart will beat in perfect honesty, transparency, and truth; its perfect place of rest and peace. The heart was meant to live in "Zion" ~ the place where God dwells. The Psalms have forty-eight references to this wonderful place (which is another word for heaven), or the ultimate dwelling place of God and His people.

THE GREATEST HIGH

Great intelligence is either developed by education, or possessing a natural high Intelligence Quotient (IQ). But an understanding mind coupled with a hearing heart comes from the Lord (1 Kings 3:9, Amp). Just like great intelligence can be used for great good, so a corrupt genius wreaks great destruction.

My reference concerning the following facts are from Romans 1:18-32. The brain, with the heart and mind, was not created to receive anything that produces a curse. The mind was meant to be a blessing to the possessor of such faculties, including it being applied for the blessing of others. Jesus paid with His blood to free us from every curse (Galatians 3:13), including the freedom from the origin of where curses are formed in the carnal (sensual) mind. Being carnally minded denies the existence of the unseen God and believes the mind is to be most depended on, highly honored and even worshipped. This leads to an obsession with self and its sensual physical needs. It leads to a lifestyle of inner-focus, selfishness and pride ~ which opposes co-operation with the Creator. Such minds would also rather respect and admire creation more so than the Creator Himself. In this way paganism is related to a worship of nature and animals. So also atheism and the anti-Christ mind are therefore formed in the carnal mind.

Additionally, carnality is a perverse mind that denies following God because following self is sufficient. Since the mind was created to imitate someone, it lands up imitating itself and that is where idolatry, homosexuality, lesbianism and "same-sex marriage" strongholds form.

Following the Lord Jesus Christ, taking up your cross and not following your own preferences, is cooperating with the Almighty God, whose mind cannot be measured or fathomed.

Take note of Jesus words in this Scripture:

Luke 9:23 (Amp)

"And He was saying to them all, "If anyone wishes to follow Me [as My disciple], he must deny himself [set aside selfish interests], and take up his cross daily [expressing a willingness to endure whatever may come] and follow Me [believing in Me, conforming to My example in living and, if need be, suffering or perhaps dying because of faith in Me]."

Becoming one in mind with Jesus is the essence of this Scripture. Through your submission to the mind of Christ you die to your personal preferences. Your desires become conformed to that of the Father and your mind becomes an asset, a benefit, and an advantage to your life and that of others. If not, it could become a liability that becomes an expensive "legal" responsibility, an accountability and charge to your healthy state of well-being.

Your mind was not granted to you as your enemy but your servant-friend that allows you to function by divine design. The mind of Christ understands how valuable the human brain is and nurtures, educates and "puts the right fuel" in it. It abstains from destructive drugs, stimulants, and even laziness that diminish the ability to give the greatest glory to the Creator.

God desires that we experience the absolute fullness of the adventure of life: to literally live and feel His love, joy, peace, passion and fulfillment that enables us to go through life's storms that are filled with hate, rejection, depression and restlessness. The covenant, passionate love of the Father enables us to be on the "greatest high" of life!

2 Samuel 22:33-35 (AMP)

"God is my strong fortress; He sets the blameless in His way. He makes my feet like the doe's feet [firm and swift]; He sets me [secure and confident] on my high places.
"He trains my hands for war, so that my arms can bend (pull back) a bow of bronze"

The Lord is that "strong fortress"~ that high and unreachable place where no enemy can reach us. He enables us to do things never done before.

The word "renew" is to produce something fresh, like serving a fresh cup of coffee. Many of my friends greatly appreciate "real" coffee,

154

and that remains a point of opinion. But there is a great difference in taste when you are serving the real thing compared to just filtering used ground coffee. You can recognize the taste of second-rate coffee but it lacks that strength, aroma or flavor that freshly ground provides. Renewing your mind, however allows you to experience the full reality of the presence of God. You are absorbing all of His glory.

Ephesians 4:17-19 (MSG)

"And so I insist—and God backs me up on this—that there be no going along with the crowd, the empty-headed, mindless crowd. They've refused for so long to deal with God that they've lost touch not only with God but with reality itself. They can't think straight anymore. Feeling no pain, they let themselves go in sexual obsession, addicted to every sort of perversion"

The wayward heart is the disobedient, willful, rebellious and defiant heart that sneers at co-operation with God. It is because the heart of love has not yet been discovered. But even after you have found His love, it is vital that the renewal of the mind is your response to cooperating with God. Do you see the vital importance of renewing your mind? What you put in your mind is what will start developing in your heart. Now look at this process. If we sow a thought, we reap an action. If we sow an action, we reap a habit. If we sow a habit, we reap a lifestyle. If we sow a lifestyle, we reap our destiny! It all starts with a thought!

I pray you see the importance of guarding your heart to cooperate with the One who only has your best interests at heart! What you allow to grow in your mind will become part of your heart, and will inevitably become your destiny. Part of guarding your heart and mind is filling your thoughts with heavenly things ~ God's thoughts. So that you will never lose hope, grow tired or weary.

Isaiah 40:31 (Amp)

"But those who wait for the Lord [who expect, look for, and hope in Him] will gain new strength and renew their power; they will lift up their wings [and rise up close to God] like eagles [rising toward the sun]; they will run and not become weary, they will walk and not grow tired"

PRODUCT OF THE HEART

Jesus revealed that what you give your time to, that what you treasure or highly regard, will become the treasure or product of your heart (Matthew 6:21). If this concept is true regarding producing good, it is also true regarding producing what is corrupt or evil.

Demonic thoughts can, however, only produce what we allow. It is therefore within the governance of our heart, or the mind of Christ, that we are able to steer the mind to His Word and restrain the mouth from anything contradictory. Meditating upon the Word of God in your thoughts, and continually confessing these thoughts could be the difference in producing either life or death.

Proverbs 18:21 (Amp)

"Death and life are in the power of the tongue, and those who love it and indulge it will eat its fruit and bear the consequences of their words"

Jesus gave this warning about perception:

Luke 8:18 (Amp)

"So be careful how you listen; for whoever has [a teachable heart], to him more [understanding] will be given; and whoever does not have [a longing for truth], even what he thinks he has will be taken away from him."

He also warned:

Matthew 12:36 (Amp)

"But I tell you, on the Day of Judgment people will have to give an accounting for every careless or useless word they speak."

EMOTIONS, PAIN AND YOUR MIND

Your mind is the door to your emotions. Your soul contains these emotions, so what happens in the mind also effects the emotions. When you feel worried, rejected, or even if you feel confident it all has to do with a mindset. When you receive bad news, you start thinking about it and that can lead to depression. You can, however, be developing the art of happiness by simply focusing on the will of God.

If it takes words to produce your happiness, then words can also produce sadness. Your mind is like a central control office that processes mindsets. It is thus very important that, despite our emotional state, we choose to enter into the mindset that is greater than ours ~ the mind of Christ. Whatever impossibility our mind is dealing with, the mind of Christ is able handle whatever comes our way. What the Holy Spirit does in such a case is to expand our mind-capacity in times of crises.

As mentioned previously the mind of Christ consists of light. It is like the proverbial light-bulb moment that comes to us when we're stuck or dealing with a problem. It is that sudden revelation or illuminations that help you figure it out. That is the Holy Spirit, which is the mind of Christ in operation!

The mind of Christ is a place of understanding, and because of it His joy resides. Your mind can unlock things that have been closed for many years. Your decision to choose joy can even bring healing to your body. You can be feeling adverse symptoms in your body, but if you condition your mind to speak to your body, it will start aligning with your confession of the promises of God.

For this reason it is vital to be aware of what we allow in our mind, for what we allow effects our emotions and likewise our bodies. Negative emotions have an invisible physical effect on our minds that, if not checked, can lead to depression, suicidal thoughts and disease.

The mind of Christ brings freedom and healing. Choose to always be thinking like God, like Christ thinks. If we can change our meditation ~ the things we focus on, what is important, what is good and of a noble source ~ we can create a happy and joyful life. Your mind is supposed to bring you happiness and also enable you to worship God.

As you were made in the image of God, your words carry life. Tell your mind to focus on Christ, and that God is going to work on your behalf. This is the mind of Christ and you can switch your thinking to His mind.

WORRY DIVIDES THE MIND

Jesus provided a Rock-solid solution to a mindless lifestyle, a life wallowing in poverty, worry and lack. In Matthew 6, He taught on the importance of resorting to prayer instead of worrying about wealth. He said that instead of keeping your mind occupied on exhausting strategies to make an income, He said we are to seek the mind of God first; to seek His kingdom first in order to receive His perfect strategies.

As mentioned before, God is all about communication. Prayer is not just giving your shopping list to God, but really falling into the arms of a Father who loves you.

From a perspective of love, your faith is restored and your mind gets cleared from worry that clouds your judgment and creativity.

Worry is really something to guard against. The Greek word for "worry" is *"merimnao"*, which comes from *"merizo"*, meaning, "to divide into parts". The word suggests a distraction, a preoccupation with things causing anxiety, stress, and pressure.

Declare a greater surrender to Jesus, the Word of God for your life. Confess a single-hearted devotion to God, bringing you freedom from fear and strength of mind. Your undivided commitment towards God stands strong against the enemy, who wants to lure you into distractions of worry and anything outside of God's will. Accept the words of Jesus: *"Is not life more than food and the body more than clothing?"* (Matt. 6:25-34). He was emphasizing having an undivided mind as a fruitful source of producing life-giving ways.

Discard any anxious thoughts as an unbecoming mindset, as a trusting representative of Christ. See yourself growing in partnership with the Lord by a closer partnership with the Holy Spirit. You will never regret being totally undivided and loyal to Him. He is seeking those whose hearts are co-operating with Him, those who are completely *for* Him and faithful to Him.

ೞ৪০

2 Chronicles 16:9 (Amp)

"For the eyes of the Lord move to and fro throughout the earth so that He may support those whose heart is completely His"

PART 3
ACTIVATING THE MIND

CHAPTER 10
ONE IN MIND

ଔଚ୪ଓ

Acts 2:1 (NKJ)

*"When the Day of Pentecost had fully come,
they were all with one accord in one place"*

An important aspect of being one with the mind of Christ is being one with His people. You would think that having an intimate encounter with the life-giving breath of Jesus would be the ultimate spiritual experience! But after He breathed on them, He told them to *get together* in Jerusalem to further await the Holy Spirit. There's something about personally receiving the breath of Jesus in the born-again experience, but there is also an *empowering* to receiving the "wind" and the "fire" of God, enabling you to both communicate and work *as one* in God.

163

These supernatural impartations from being in unity with the Lord Jesus Himself are vital for the healthy operation and growth of His church and the result of being united with Him. Being one with Jesus by His Spirit *enables* us to be united as a body of believers.

Jesus breathed on His disciples to receive His Spirit, and only then were they ready to work as one with other believers. The reason for Jesus *not* commissioning His disciples right away after He breathed on them was because He wanted that outpouring of His passion to be a corporate impartation.

In Acts 2:1 they were *"all with one accord in one place"* when the Pentecostal outpouring took place. This was only the beginning and the original spark from which the Christian mind operates. Without this experience in a believer's personal life there will always be limited understanding of the truths of God, and limited effectiveness in the work of the Gospel in the lives of others.

I've been ministering throughout the world since the age of sixteen and I am a living testimony of the power of the Holy Spirit, and how this concept is a vital necessity to adopt as a mindset for all Christians worldwide. Even through my missions' training and all the experiences of teaching, preaching and ministering healing to people, they are nothing compared to the united efforts of a believing group that has the Holy Spirit power to bring about healing and change.

Pastor Richard reported that his sister was healed recently from scoliosis. She'd had this disease since childhood and no one knew that she'd suffered from this. During our revival time in San Francisco at a Place to Meet Jesus, she was completely healed through the anointing of corporate worship and the receiving of revelatory preaching. She remains healed to this day and reports, "It feels so good to have the use of my back without pain!"

Throughout the Old Testament God *visited* His people by placing His Spirit *upon* His children. Now, He wants to *inhabit* all people individually and communally by abiding *in* us. He asks us to respond to *"abide in Me"* like the branch is to the vine (John 15). When Jesus prayed for us in the Garden of Gethsemane in John 17, He prayed that we should be both one with the Father and also be one with one another.

THE PURPOSE OF UNITY

In Acts 2:2-4, the corporate outpouring of the Spirit occurred in the form of three outward, and inward, manifestations: *"rushing, mighty wind"*; *"divided tongues of fire"* and the ability to *"speak with other tongues"*. In each of these three demonstrations, we find the purpose of

165

God to passionately unite believers with Him and with others.

These inner and outer manifestations can be interpreted as the three ways the Holy Spirit expresses Himself: audibly, visibly, and in our understanding. He however is not limited to just these expressions.

On this occasion He announced His arrival with the sound of a "rushing, violent wind" upon the building. Then manifesting in a flame of fire, He defused the believers entirely by "lighting them up" ~ the flame was seen dividing up and lighting upon each person's head as if to mark each one. We can really elaborate greatly on the symbolism and meaning of these elements, but my main point is that God wanted to unite us for communication. This act of grace in which He for the first time inhabited the bodies of believers, was marked with a new language. They were given the ability to not only communicate with God but to *commune* with Him without the limitations of language. What transpired was so unusual, the only sense people could make of it was that the disciples were intoxicated. But the work of the Holy Spirit was validated in that these infused people were granted supernaturally to be able to *communicate* with people from visiting countries without having to learn their language!

These gifts are still available today for all those with open hearts and minds, who understand the purpose of God's love in them. They will develop our unified hearts with God and with believers He has assigned us to.

He is manifesting Himself all over the world, but not where there is unbelief or where He is being limited. Unite with believers who are dedicated to this unified voice of the Lord.

LOVE ABOVE HURT

Sometimes keeping and building unity can be hindered by intense hurt and offence. Even though relational challenges are inevitable, the worst stance to take in such a case is accepting the effects of it in your heart and mind. Many individuals, including groups of people in both private and public capacities who do not value the principle of unity, stunt relational and spiritual advancement, including effective productivity. You can have peace, but unity is something that comes about when (without judgment) "speaking the truth in love". It is the antidote to having such a situation be left alone to fester.

Ephesians 4:15 (Amp)

"But speaking the truth in love [in all things—both our speech and our lives expressing His truth], let us grow up in all things into Him [following His example] who is the Head—Christ"

Activating your mind in Christ is activating your awareness of unity. Many families hold grudges or offences and forfeit trust and meaningful truthful relationships because they do not risk the *process* that unity requires.

They believe it is okay for emotional hurts to be "swept under the rug" and undervalue the counsel of the Holy Spirit through trained and mature pastoral care. This is both ignorance and deception. This stronghold leads to bearing inevitable, destructive fruit, no matter what measures are taken to ignore or avoid it. Both physical and emotional hurts are part of life, but unity with genuine pastoral leadership allows the healing anointing of the Holy Spirit to restore unity. A key Scripture emphasizes this:

Psalm 133 (MSG)

"How wonderful, how beautiful, when brothers and sisters get along! It's like costly anointing oil flowing down head and beard, flowing down Aaron's beard, flowing down the collar of his priestly robes. It's like the dew on Mount Hermon flowing down the slopes of Zion. Yes, that's where God commands the blessing, ordains eternal life."

When God commands a blessing, no one can revoke or challenge it. As we cooperate with God to bring unity in our families, churches, and nations, we usher in the anointing of servant-leadership that covers and protects both man and property.

As you gather your mindset of becoming an agent of reconciliation wherever you go, you are bringing great blessing and kingdom advancement. Through this residing anointing people will remain comforted, cleansed, wrapped and allowed to be nursed and healed.

The mind of Christ is a mind that brings wholeness and healing, not division and enmity. If unity is welcomed, love will abide. We can only do so by applying the mind of Jesus.

2 Corinthians 5:18 (AMP)

"But all these things are from God, who reconciled us to Himself through Christ [making us acceptable to Him] and gave us the ministry of reconciliation [so that by our example we might bring others to Him]"

THE LIFESTYLE OF FORGIVENESS

It is almost impossible to touch the subject of unity without touching love and forgiveness. Forgiveness not only sparks unity but it maintains the healing process that hurt brings. That is why it has to be applied in progressive and consistent sessions within the mind.

Matthew 18:21-22 (AMP)

"Then Peter came to Him and asked, 'Lord, how many times will my brother sin against me and I forgive him and let it go? Up to seven times?' Jesus answered him, 'I say to you, not up to seven times, but seventy times seven'"

169

True forgiveness through reconciliation doesn't only release the hurt, but it also deals with the hurt that the *intent* has caused. If someone bumped into you accidentally, intentional hurt was not the motive and a simple apology should be sufficient.

But if someone *intentionally* planned a vendetta of revenge or harm against you, the process of reconciliation is necessary should that relationship be one God requires. That is why intentional hurt is dealt with by intentional forgiveness, of which so few have the emotional stamina for. It takes a process of *choosing* to love like God does, and applying the powerful process of His covenant love to the rebellious mind. Declaring reconciliation through forgiveness is not a one-time occasion, but a steady process of reinforcement, which has to be applied to the mind each time hurt or resentment wants to find a foothold. The tree of forgiveness is a seed that has to be watered and nurtured for the fruit of love to grow ~ or it will grow into a destructive foreign entity that has to eventually be painfully eradicated. Embrace forgiveness that leads to unity, as a means to gain the mind of Christ, the character of Christ"

Ephesians 4:13 (NKJV)

"Till we all come to the unity of the faith and of the knowledge of the Son of God, to a perfect man, to the measure of the stature of the fullness of Christ"

Once again, unity and reconciliation are things that are only accomplished by the powerful force of the Holy Spirit operating through a heart of faith. A believer from South Africa gave testimony of this process when he was going through a phase of relational trauma and rejection in ministry.

He was in a daily habit of spending time with the Lord while taking his morning shower. In these vulnerable moments, the Lord directed him to a condition of resentment in his heart, and that he needed to pursue forgiveness to stay "clean" before the Lord.

As the warm water flooded over his head and body, he visualized the love and forgiveness of God covering him completely, causing the man to release the resentment and forgive those who had hurt him. He felt refreshed and washed after his session with God. The next day, as he was seeking the Lord again in the shower, he realized that that "clean feeling" had waned and that he was still harboring hurt as resentment was still visiting him. As he prayed for direction the "still small voice" came to his consciousness.

As the water again washed over him, the voice of God flooded his heart and he knew that he was okay with doing this every day for the rest of his life. As much as he would need to take a shower daily for the rest of his life, he would also need to forgive those who hurt him daily for as long as he lived. He told me that even though this was very difficult for him to do, it brought him closer to the heart of God and it has somehow enlarged his heart for people too!

As we nurture the love-based thoughts of Christ we start acting from His heart, no matter how difficult or uncomfortable it might seem.

The heart and mind of Christ requires and acquires a heart of obedience, which disallows anything to attach and burden the heart other than the love of God itself. Disunity, unforgiveness, and resentment cannot abide in the heart that is pursuing the love of God.

UNITY IN SERVANTHOOD

The covenant love of God in the heart has no room for personal ego. In a marriage two people love each other from their soul realms and from their minds. Though they are physically attracted to each other and have made conscious decisions to remain committed, there still is an emotional high from being in love. They also admire their partner's intellect, which make them both feel loved, but this is not where the maturity of true love ends.

The unconditional covenant love of God brings a marriage into spiritual maturity, which transcends all emotional experiences. An unbreakable spiritual bond occurs in a family or a friendship, where love in *servant's attitude* is demonstrated, where the goal is to love like God does ~ and where the focus is on becoming spiritually one with the other person.

It is not only our *obedience* that leads us into a life of love, but it's our *duty* to be walking in the mindset of humble unity with the mind of Christ. Servanthood is the greatest mindset Jesus requires ~ and that includes really taking interest and caring for family, friends, neighborhood, and country.

Love is not a competition; it is an attitude of childlike faith in *God* while caring for others.

Matthew 18:4 (NKJV)

"Therefore whoever humbles himself as this little child is the greatest in the kingdom of heaven"

The mind of Christ is not only heavenly but it is realistic, it is applicable to daily abundant living. One cannot remain in the unrealistic mindset that guards itself from the hurt of relationships. We cannot remain in a self-preservation mindset that gets stuck in pessimism and suspicion. You must come to a place that wherever you find yourself, you are fully leaning on God's help to trust others (since you are uniting with the mindset of Christ) that everybody deserves to be blessed. God desires to include everyone who welcomes Him through you.

I pray you would allow God to defend you and to bring you justice, for evil will surely be exposed. Take the responsibility to purely find the good in people. May stereotyping, or prejudice bringing blindness, be far from your thinking. Allow God to show you how *He* sees people. You will start enjoying their company and feel His joy for them. May you develop a thought life of joy and delight in others, maximizing the moments God gives. May His love develop a love tolerance for others.

1 Corinthians 13:9 (Msg)

"Love... puts up with anything, trusts God always, always looks for the best, never looks back, but keeps going to the end"

GLORY AND SUFFERING

Colossians 1:27 (Amp)

"God [in His eternal plan] chose to make known to them how great for the Gentiles are the riches of the glory of this mystery, which is Christ in and among you, the hope and guarantee of [realizing the] glory"

Christ in you manifests love in thought and action. This is the glory of God demonstrated and the hope of glory maintained. As unity develops through loving servanthood, the reality of the glory of God increases bringing the *realization* that becoming great in God is part of becoming mature in Him. With this knowledge, the Apostle Paul taught the *necessity* of developing a hope of greatness for all mankind. The mind of Christ grants you the *development* of hope through a clean conscience but also provides the *capacity* of living to the glory of God.

Doing what Jesus requires of you goes beyond your human capacity. It is never easy or convenient, but it will grant you living within your life purpose ~ to give great glory to Him. Consider that your natural mind will not take kindly to accepting the commitment to be living for both His glory and also the things He suffered (Phil. 3:10).

"More of Him and less of me" is the manifestation of the mind of Christ ~ it is solely committed to making Him Lord in all things.

In our humanity we can grow complacent or familiar with this glory ~ in both the giving of it and the consciousness of living within it. My prayer is that we will be determined to continue finding ways to faithfully honor the glory of God by simply loving Him and obeying Him within our thinking. This comes with a lifestyle of thankfulness, an acceptance and a gratefulness of Him sharing His glory with you.

In so doing, we also recognize the glory of God upon others and we aim to be an encouragement to that person as a means of granting even greater glory to the Lord. The key is to not do it in a manner that will bring a spotlight upon that person, but allow that person to turn the spotlight on the Lord. We do not exclusively gain someone's favor by honoring them, for that will breed pride. But giving more glory to the Lord by encouraging them will build someone else's faith in God.

Psalm 16:2-3 (NKJV)

"O my soul, you have said to the Lord, you are my Lord, my goodness is nothing apart from You. As for the saints who are on the earth, they are the excellent ones, in whom is all my delight"

CAPACITY FOR GREATNESS

I recognize a great need in the Body of Christ, for the unified mindset of pure honor. The glory of God resides in believing saints and that is why we cannot have a mindset to disregard or avoid showing them honor. We also cannot disregard the inheritance of favor or think of ourselves unfit for the glorious riches of His blessings.

If you are in Christ the mindset of being honorable and excellent is not something you have *deserved,* but it has been bestowed upon you by *grace*. That is why we humbly and discreetly wear the honor of Christ within. It is a "uniform" we wear with His great grace, enabling us to extend appropriate honor to others.

Psalm 84:11 (NKJV)

"For the Lord God is a sun and shield; The Lord will give grace and glory; no good thing will He withhold from those who walk uprightly"

If you are complimented or encouraged, receive that honor with true humility and elegance and not with awkwardness or false humility, for that is unbelief. As a representative of the kingdom you have the mind of the culture of kingdom honor. It is not you to judge whether honor is due to you or grow resentful if honor is being withheld. For this is a mystery and a secret part of your intimate relationship with Him.

In Matthew chapter 6, Jesus focuses on the posture and attitude of our communion with God. From a vertical life of giving prayer and worship, a horizontal giving occurs.

It is, however, important to operate within the appropriate method. Jesus teaches *how* to handle the giving of a "charitable deed". I believe this lesson covers all manner of giving, even that of giving words of encouragement or honor. The prerequisite of being "open-

177

handed," is that the attention should not be placed upon you but on the *glory of God*. We can, therefore, be a little more creative when it comes to giving gifts, complimenting or honoring all people. There is much glory in anonymous giving, encouragement, and love shown, as this places the deserving glory upon God.

As much as you recognize honorable people by being honorable yourself, you are also able to *be* such within your *environment*. Wherever you go and whatever you do, you sow the glory of God and the glory of His mercies in that place. Whether you are renting a home, visiting a hotel room, or shopping, your public presence gives you a representation to live honorably.

You are a heavenly ambassador and thereby hold kingly stature in the Spirit. What's more, great people have organized, clean homes that enable their hospitality to become a haven for ministry.

Matthew 5:14-15 (Amp)

"You are the light of [Christ to] the world. A city set on a hill cannot be hidden; nor does anyone light a lamp and put it under a basket, but on a lampstand, and it gives light to all who are in the house"

Many people are not able to grow in the mindset of greatness of the Lord because they do not know how to build capacity for it ~ how to accommodate it. Consider the truth of Jesus' words above. As mentioned before, because Christ is within you have the *"hope for glory"*! You *are "the light of the world"* ~ you were meant to shine and be placed in an elevated noticeable place in life for the glory of God. This is most definitely for benefit of *others*, not only for you. This also means honoring leadership, and government officials are part of that responsibility. Recognize that no matter how undeserving they might be, God places authorities in power ~ and part of agreeing with His kingdom is living within the honor of those He has placed over you. Pure honor, therefore, combats rebellion and lives without fear.

Reject self-pity. Do not divert your attention from this truth by thinking this glory belongs to somebody else more worthy. The covenant of Christ with you has made you commendable! Identify and shed the mindsets that cultural disadvantage, poor upbringing, or lack of education has limited you, and embrace the truth that you were destined for greatness.

In addition, we have all been created in the equal image of God. All prerequisites, conditions, or qualification factors are unnecessary since Christ has already attained your identity in Him to be one with the Father. We all carry the same power and the same image. That is why we need to appreciate and honor one another, regardless of race, background, or reputation. The mind of Christ grows in the capacity for greatness.

HONOUR VERSUS SUPERIORITY

When Christians enter a broader leadership scope, there can be controversy because of envy or jealousy. There can also be a mask of envy mistakenly called "discernment". This is below the privileges of the Spirit-filled children of God!

There should be an even greater culture of honor because he or she is not just a normal person, but someone who has extra senses that only the Spirit of God provides.

1 Corinthians 2:14 (MSG)

"The unspiritual self, just as it is by nature, can't receive the gifts of God's Spirit. There's no capacity for them. They seem like so much silliness. Spirit can be known only by spirit—God's Spirit and our spirits in open communion. Spiritually alive, we have access to everything God's Spirit is doing, and can't be judged by unspiritual critics. Isaiah's question, 'Is there anyone around who knows God's Spirit, anyone who knows what he is doing?' has been answered: Christ knows, and we have Christ's Spirit."

If you see a fellow Christian advancing, like running for political office or getting a leadership promotion at work, your faith should not primarily be in the *person*, but the recognition of God's *Spirit inside* that person. At that very minute your co-operation concerning the leadership God has instituted for your benefit is a commitment to make before the Lord. In this way, we also carry a burden together, which makes that person's obedience to God so much more effective.

Luke 2:52 (NKJV)

"And Jesus kept increasing in wisdom and in stature, and in favor with God and men"

I pray you will start understanding that you have the capacity of increasing glory radiating from your life. Those who have been given the capacity to be visible in the public eye, like musicians, actors and artists, are mostly suffering under the spirit of envy. Let us continue, by the wisdom of the Lord, to encourage and share the joy of shining for Christ.

COLLECTIVE GREATNESS NOW

In order for us to appreciate this greatness in one another, we need to begin to see *ourselves* becoming that person who is able to accommodate the glory of God.

Many believers are so crippled by circumstances and unbelief. They only see the past and regard their present problems as permanent. The Lord wants to lift your head and your eyes to see the eternal state of blessing God has in mind. He wants you to think eternally and recognize you are only a pilgrim here, journeying through today to get to tomorrow's blessing. David had a revelation of this:

Psalm 3:2-4 (AMP)

"Many are saying of me, 'There is no help [no salvation] for him in God.' Selah. But You, O LORD, are a shield for me, my glory [and my honor], and the One who lifts my head. With my voice I was crying to the LORD, and He answered me from His holy mountain. Selah."

See beyond your circumstance today and recognize the glory of God poured out to you now. Recognize today that God is your total defense and shield in any circumstance. You are, therefore, able to lift your chin, able to see beyond the present. The Holy Spirit is about to reveal that heavenly vision of total restoration, healing, and reformation in your life and mind.

Just like David, heed the invitation to call upon the Lord and He will answer *"from His holy mountain"*. The Lord's mountain is His stronghold. It is the place where we receive His strength, His Word ~ through intentional times of study, meditation, and prayer. Calling upon Him is your daily strength to fight the good fight of remaining in faith (2 Tim. 4:7).

Through a genuine connection with the Lord in prayer, your faith will be replenished, and He will also take you to that reality where you start confessing and believing that truth. You will most definitely walk in His destiny and arrive *at* that destination. But first, He will lead you through your *sense* of having destiny.

Speaking forth the vision of God as a reality is an ancient, holy principle ~ and you share the ability and power of it. When the earth was *"formless and void"* (Gen 1:1), the vision of God for the earth was present but not complete.

You are no longer devoid of greatness because you have not allowed your life to remain shapeless or unstructured. You have received the Word and vision of God in your mind and mouth to transform that void, to make your life valid and significant. You were meant for greatness, you were meant to shine for the glory of God!

Isaiah 60:1 (NKJV)

"Arise; shine; for your light has come! And the glory of the Lord is risen upon you"

Take an uninterrupted moment to dedicate time to the Lord. Allow His Spirit during this time to hover and brood over you to dispel all darkness from your thinking. You will only be able to truly see the reality of life when you have received both His love and the greatness that His love forms within.

When you start unifying with God, you start agreeing with Him. You agree by decreeing His vision into existence for your life. Decreeing His vision is ruling in His kingdom, it is announcing the verdict of hope of God's glory poured out on your life. It is the declaration that you do not live under judgment, but live under the *order* of God by His Spirit. You do not request the enemy to leave, but you command and insist upon it! You remember how great He is and you understand He has meant to share this greatness with *you*. The mind of Christ agrees with God and lives within that greatness.

೦ತಿಐ

CHAPTER 11
WISDOM OF
HOLY SPIRIT COUNSEL
ೞ

Isaiah 9:6 (AMP)

"For to us a Child shall be born, to us a Son shall be given; and the government shall be upon His shoulder, and His name shall be called Wonderful, Counselor, Mighty God, Everlasting Father, Prince of Peace"

SPIRIT OF COUNSEL

If you are someone who has much gifting and potential but you are really wrestling through some issues in your ministry, the pivotal point is not in the doing the next logical thing, but aligning your mindset and thoughts to the Lord in prayer. As you connect with Him as your Counselor, you come into the mind of Christ for your situation.

The "Spirit of Counsel" (Isaiah 11:2) is one of the attributes of the Holy Spirit occupying your mind in Christ.

185

It is the ability to have understanding, knowledge and insight. It grants you perception, an astuteness and intelligence far above your natural ability. It grants you good judgment and an ability to penetrate riddles and mysteries, interpret visions dreams and prophetic direction. Most importantly, it leads you away from the path of foolishness, which at its core is thoughtlessness.

In His abiding presence you will find this wisdom. You only need to ask for it by unswerving faith. James 1:5-8 promises that God will grant it without reserve. Many people pray only for provision, but we learn from Solomon that praying for wisdom is a better prayer. God wants to draw you to Him and mature you at the same time. He will grant you the thinking patterns that will propel you to your prophetic destiny. As I confess the vibrant, prophetic truths in prayer before the Lord, I find an inner dynamo starting up ~ a vigor that was not there before, projecting me towards a greater vision in Him. He provides the superior counsel of heaven.

COUNSEL WITH OTHERS

As you forsake anxiety and walk in the peace His presence provides, the Lord will sometimes direct you to seek counsel from the wise. He is ready to confirm and expand the wisdom that is due to you in the natural.

As Jesus increased in favor with both God and man (Luke 2:52), you will be able to both discern this inner wisdom, including who are of good counsel within the sphere of your assignment.

God has various supernatural means to place these wise relationships in your company. Only if need be should you seek them out, for your job is to maintain the *peace* of the Lord. The Bible describes this inner peace as one that passes understanding. This is so that you will recognize intuitively the relationships He presents to you.

Philippians 4:6-7 (Amp)

"Do not be anxious or worried about anything, but in everything [every circumstance and situation] by prayer and petition with thanksgiving, continue to make your [specific] requests known to God. And the peace of God [that peace which reassures the heart, that peace] which transcends all understanding, [that peace which] stands guard over your hearts and your minds in Christ Jesus [is yours]"

It is therefore vital that you do not allow discouragement, depression, or introversion during these times when faith is required. God is directing you to wiser paths. God is advancing in you. He always has something better in mind for you and places to go where you've never been. Ask the Lord to lead you to these new and open doors. You will know the *right path* through inner peace, as you trust the

Lord to lead you daily, and place His assignment steps in front of you.

This peace will also help you discern those who are not meant to walk with you, who might hinder your progress. It is unrealistic to think everyone you meet is meant to be part of your life. The Lord will grant you the love and wisdom on how to either avoid them or gently let them go. If you know you get easily distracted or you're in a busy period of life, free up your schedule to enable you to be more focused on the wise voice of the Lord.

Even Mary the mother of Jesus intuitively knew that she needed to connect with Elizabeth when her pregnancy was about full-term. Elizabeth, being in her second-term carrying John the Baptist, was ready to inspire and encourage her to birth the son of God because they both realized they were carrying related destinies. Get ready to be connected to your true spiritual tribe who hold the spirit of counsel and wisdom!

You don't have to quit your job or ministry in times of rejection, sickness, or stress. As much as you have the capacity to know when to act and to advance, you also have the wise mind of Christ to know when to rest, slow down, take a breath, and wait. You have the mental capacity and the strategy from the living God to allow you to lift your head and see the salvation the Lord has prepared for you. It is unique, it is personal, and it is absolutely perfect ~ for His ways are flawless and ideal. No matter what it looks like right now, what He has started He will surely complete in you!

And He will always start with renewing your mind, to cause you to fulfill that great commission He has placed on your heart.

RELATIONAL INTEGRITY

The loving God aligns our minds concerning keeping our relationships pure, so we can really connect with hearts of those around us. Relationships will be so much healthier at home, at church, and in the workplace when we pay attention to the motive and content of conversations as were led by the Holy Spirit. Poor modern lifestyle practices have been a great contributing factor towards lazy listening.

It has now become a common saying that it is no longer distance that separates us, but silence. This has become a common modern vice, since there is so much technological advancement taking over our daily thought patterns. It is no wonder after a day of texting, e-mailing or Tweeting that we are too exhausted to be communicating to our close circle: our spouse, family, children, and friends.

Which communications, and what form, are most important to you? The Holy Spirit's wisdom will help us prioritize them. Since He is our Counselor (*"Parakletos"* in the Greek ~ John 14:16), we partner with Him in discernment, not in judgment regarding words. The moment we have a superiority of heart about someone's communication, we know we are to guard against harmful judgmental conclusions.

The words of James, encouraging us to be quick to listen and slow to speak (James 1:19), are still relevant to us in the maze of communications coming to our daily lives.

Now, more than ever, we are to *really* understand the power of our thoughts and to be more selective than ever before, as to how we want to receive and sow them. This determines the outcome and fruit of our lives. Jesus brought about this principle:

Luke 6:45 (Amp)

"The [intrinsically] good man produces what is good and honorable and moral out of the good treasure [stored] in his heart; and the [intrinsically] evil man produces what is wicked and depraved out of the evil [in his heart]; for his mouth speaks from the overflow of his heart"

The mind of Christ is your inherent, built-in and essential way of thinking. It is fundamental to your focus and central to your lifestyle. As you take His word to heart you are intentionally producing and cultivating Emmanuel, "God with us".

Whether it is consciously or subconsciously, words reside in your heart. Take note of how simply your *words* will reveal the recesses of your heart. Take note of your ability to really *listen* ~ as spiritual discernment is intentionally *learned*, a skill honed over time.

I declare that your heart is the seat of Christ and that your mind is in genuine partnership with the Holy Spirit. Meditate upon your transformation into the mind in Christ, from which you will produce life. Getting the mind of Christ is intentional at first, but it will soon become a natural and genuine way of operating.

ADVANCEMENT BY WISDOM

All successful groups and companies have formed a movement or a following by the wisdom of a united mindset ~ a singular vision that brings about action. Very little has ever been accomplished by one person working alone on a vision.

According to the documented structure of the first church in the book of Acts, this collaborative mindset was formed around the commission of Christ to win souls. A collective agreement was formed around that vision to form the church of God that came about by renewed minds and reformed attitudes. The collective and united church has, for over two thousand years, been successful in bringing many souls to the Lord Jesus. But there needs to be greater advancements as world population increases. We should be on the cutting edge of spiritual advancement beyond just "winning" souls. This will happen by the wisdom of God.

Jesus' great focus was modeling His life to people as "*the Light of the world*" (John 8:12). In really advancing from mere success to great significance, we are to co-labor with the Holy Spirit's mind to expand our vision from just "catching fish" or winning souls. Jesus made us *"fishers of men,"* but He also modeled Himself as the Great Shepherd and called us, like John, to really prove our love to Him by *"shepherding the sheep"* He places before us.

Take a moment to decree that you are in the process of thinking dependently upon the Lord. Focus daily on investing your time, talent, and treasure into souls as a means to advance the kingdom of God. With this priority all your needs will be met. See yourself growing past the elementary things of the Spirit and be open to growing in the things of love. This is what mostly matters to the Lord, and it is wisdom in action.

Matthew 6:33 (AMP)

"But first and most importantly seek (aim at, strive after) His kingdom and His righteousness [His way of doing and being right—the attitude and character of God], and all these things will be given to you also"

ෆෂ෨

CHAPTER 12
CROSSROADS OF THOUGHT

ⓒ⃰ℰ⃰

Philippians 3:17-19 (Msg)

"Stick with me, friends. Keep track of those you see running this same course, headed for this same goal. There are many out there taking other paths, choosing other goals, and trying to get you to go along with them... all they want is easy street. They hate Christ's Cross. But easy street is a dead-end street"

Before embarking on a travel destination many decisions have to be made. But the most important are knowing your destination and planning your route. Once you're set in this, any unexpected deviation on the journey or unplanned crossroads, only become problems if you become disorientated and your destination is clouded.

The paths of thought occur in a similar manner. If you do not line up your thoughts with the mind of Christ, you will land up repeating the same independent destructive paths of thought like the Israelites did. Instead of their destination taking them a few weeks to reach, they ended up spending forty years in the wilderness. Following Christ in a committed relationship leads you to your life's divine destiny. It doesn't waste time proving credentials or looking good. Paul warned the Philippians about this process that diverts "robust Christianity:"

Philippians 3:12-14 (Msg)

"I'm not saying that I have this all together, that I have it made. But I am well on my way, reaching out for Christ, who has so wondrously reached out for me. Friends, don't get me wrong: By no means do I count myself an expert in all of this, but I've got my eye on the goal, where God is beckoning us onward—to Jesus. I'm off and running, and I'm not turning back."

THE PATHS OF THOUGHT

What are you imagining about your future? Your imagination originates from an idea, which then becomes a reality. Our ultimate destination is heaven, but we have paths to follow ~ especially paths of thought that lead us onward.

What your mind picks up is what you eventually will start imagining.

And what you imagine is what you eventually will be doing and ultimately become. Usually an idea gives you a thought that leads you from point A to B. But an independent imagination can lead you to many diversions from the destination.

What you imagine should not be picked up from just any source. Your mind in Christ is that constant and peaceful guard that disallows harmful imaginations from coming into your senses. Sometimes we have to start in the natural to train our spiritual consciousness. Take an uninterrupted moment to dedicate your sense of sight, hearing, smell, taste and touch to the Lord. Since you have been declared holy through your covenant with Christ, your mind in Christ is the guard that is posted to keep any foreign and unwelcome images, words, food or other substance from your person. The Old Testament priests anointed parts of their body as a means to consciously dedicate the "entry points" to God alone. Holiness is still a New Covenant requirement.

What you allow to illegitimately form part of your environment and thinking will disorientate and cloud your focus. Your intimate connection with the Spirit of God is what inspires your imagination and grants you prophetic vision within the pure will of God. Do some "housekeeping" today by hearing where you can by excluding bad habits so you can include new ones in your life. The destiny of God is grander and greater than your own thoughts or imaginations.

Therefore stand within those perimeters that the Word of God supports. When you apply the mind of Christ you are thus within the boundaries of God's liberating will. But you don't have to be afraid to think beyond what you know, because the Spirit of God can take you into zones beyond your expectations. Expect Him to inspire your imagination by faith. You will then begin to understand things that no book or teaching can make you understand because you're tapping from the mind of Jesus.

Most people don't realize that you can have an advantage in life by applying the mind of Christ. It is greater than any source of knowledge, experience, or information you can put your hands on. It is a mystery, a deep and rich treasure, all locked up in the mind of Christ ~ leading to everlasting life.

THE PILGRIMAGE HAS A DESTINATION

Once you've chosen the right path of thinking, you are given a key of faith to access the mind of Christ because you have been given access to His person. It is not a knowledge that you access through your consciousness or learn by studying. His path of thinking needs to be exchanged for knowledge of His embrace, and you simply living within the advantages of that all-encompassing love. This is a pilgrimage leading to your destination of truly and personally knowing Him.

Philippians 3:7-9 (MSG)

"The very credentials these people are waving around as something special, I'm tearing up and throwing out with the trash—along with everything else I used to take credit for. And why? Because of Christ. Yes, all the things I once thought were so important are gone from my life. Compared to the high privilege of knowing Christ Jesus as my Master, firsthand, everything I once thought I had going for me is insignificant—dog dung. I've dumped it all in the trash so that I could embrace Christ and be embraced by Him. I didn't want some petty, inferior brand of righteousness that comes from keeping a list of rules when I could get the robust kind that comes from trusting Christ— God's righteousness"

Remember, accessing the mind of Christ will always properly orientate you and lead you to a great destiny. It will build you and help you grow. With it you will also build people around you, to transform and restore your world. It will give you access to invisible realms and dimensions that can only be seen with the eyes of your spiritually-inspired imagination, which will enable you to practice it in the natural. Because you are dealing with the Creator, who is greater than all sciences, (chemistry, physics, etc.) you are dealing with the God who created the visible and the invisible. You therefore, have been given access to Him, a key to His mind, to unlock the things of the natural and supernatural through praying in His name and believing His Word.

It is also a guided process of the Holy Spirit, since He knows the human tendency to depend on self-righteousness.

MINDLESS PATHS

Many people struggle with poverty and sickness because of this one simple fact: mindless, mediocre thinking. Some have willingly conformed to carnal, corrupt thinking patterns and so timidly follow the crowd to the most comfortable route: the idols of the day. Where is the off-switch to this terrible vice growing stronger each year? The mind of Christ is the most wholesome thought path.

Let us look at how far we've fallen, which has caused us to switch our minds off to God and tuned in to idols. Man was created to worship something, and if it is not God, a substitute is accepted. The rate and scope of advancing technology plays a large part in this. The abundant availability of movies, social media, satellite television, and so on, has in many cases taken the place of time with God and with other people.

Many have mindlessly allowed themselves to be demonically programmed by substituting virtual life for the real thing. The incessant availability of Hollywood movies has saturated the minds of large groups of people. Since it is so on-hand and so easy to access, we have relented to hours and hours of daily watching for years, and it has escalated to viral proportions.

Entertainment is always in our living rooms. At the flick of a switch it has become our focus, our comfort, and our source of joy. In most homes people are so lonely they have to switch the television on to "feel at home", even though everyone's home. In their success in creating these idols of society, they have managed to drift from the Lord, who has created us to find our primary focus ~ comfort and joy in Him.

We also know that all kinds of other addictions in our modern society have caused our minds to become self-focused and thus switched off to spirituality. We see so many cultural norms becoming a slow-suicide of the masses. God created us to communicate, to care, and to love. We need to become a lot more vigilant towards eliminating destructive things we allow and tolerate in our lives.

The biggest concern, however, is the age-old problem that the youngest and most innocent always suffer the most from society's problems because the addictions I mentioned don't only target free-willed adults. We have an onslaught of addiction programmed from infancy ~ the dependence on "screens". I'm talking about television, computer monitors, and phones.

Did you know that within satanic circles, the greatest purpose for any coven targeting a victim is to evoke suicide? Yes, the devil is not out to play. He is literally out to kill minds and lives, and he loves to shift the blame onto our very own decisions!

Like a deadly cancer developing, the use of screen technology hardly skips the best of us. This is since indulgence also means the convenience of information, even the means of income. Monitoring world markets; downloading the latest movies, TV series, documentaries; access to social networking, has made the reality of life a little less daunting for most ~ but for others it has made them completely lose touch with reality.

Of course, very "*good*" excuses are offered to justify being glued to television. It's better than to be engaged in other vices like drugs and alcohol. But basically they are all addictions of the mind. They are replacing the essence of man ~ to communicate, and to enjoy giving and receiving love. This too affects a real and lasting relationship with the Creator and Lover of our souls.

Do you see the strategy of Satan against your mind? Do you see that he is first after your mind before he will get near your person or what you've built for yourself? Do you see that the greatest enemy of our souls is mindlessness? I've taken the time to highlight this way of thinking since it is the greatest challenge we are facing in modern living. That is why this book is so important to each and every believer who desires breakthrough for their lives and those of others.

In November 2013, a woman attending our Friday meetings in California had come from Egypt.

She said she no longer wanted to live due to the severe physical pain she was living with. After time in worship, prayer, and the Word, she testified that her entire body was healed and was excited because she would now live a pain-free life by the grace of the Holy Spirit. This is available to you today! You don't always need someone to pray for you, as your mind in Christ allows you to bring your petitions before the Father to give you access to quality of life.

John 15:7 (NKJV)

"If you abide in Me, and My words abide in you, you will ask what you desire, and it shall be done for you"

CHOOSE THE PATH TENACIOUSLY

Mindsets are formed and shaped through past experiences ~ but the mind has the ability to form thoughts *within* those experiences that are either life giving or destructive. You have the power to *choose* which way your thoughts will go.

Businessmen who know the importance of tenacity in acquiring a deal use an example of this process. They know that persistence in business will grant them the opportunities and experiences that bring reward. Despite failures and resistance, they have developed a tenacity that brings prosperity. Certain politicians who have honed the power of vision by sharing persuasive information with their voters use the same strategy.

You can really learn from experienced business and marketing people how to strategize your thinking towards success. I pray you will welcome expanded ways of thinking in faith by connecting with sound business people in your life. It will expand your faith and challenge small-mindedness.

Matthew 7:7 (NKJV)

"Ask, and it will be given to you; seek, and you will find; knock, and it will be opened to you"

BREAK LIMITATIONS

The indwelling Holy Spirit supersedes the limitations of your mind. As you partner with Him, He teaches you to be thinking about what *He* can do, and not what *you* can do.

Now that we know Jesus has bought us to breakthrough, united thinking, and what His thoughts are towards us, let us identify the things that cause independent mediocre thinking.

A story of the late Dr. Myles Monroe illustrates this, when he was loaned a Mercedes to drive on Germany's Autobahn for the first time. The Autobahn is the only highway in the world that has no speed limit. As he was reaching 100 miles per hour he noticed an Audi passing him. Only then did he only realize the unnecessary limit he was putting on his accelerator.

As he compared the capacity of the Audi to his Mercedes, he was annoyed that he hadn't been aware of its an untapped speed advantage.

When he looked down at his speedometer he was astounded that he car could reach a maximum of 300 miles per hour, and thought how small-minded he had been to only choose 100 miles per hour. He realized it was only the disciplined mindset of his home country that prohibited him from experiencing higher speeds. Being in another country with a limitless law gave him the freedom to reach speeds he never thought possible.

You may have been given freedom but your mind may limit you because of the things you have heard and taught. Ask the Lord to remove the limits of you mind and to place your foot on the accelerator of faith. You will know no limits in God!

You might think you only have a capacity of an Audi vehicle, but if you know how to use your freedom to its maximum potential you will also benefit as much as a person who has the capacity of a Mercedes!

Is it not true that certain people who have had education at the best universities are still not using their full knowledge and potential ~ that they are still poor and depressed? Solomon said that you could have the most powerful horse, but you will never know its power if you stay seated in a chariot. You don't have to be super smart or wealthy to achieve success.

You only need to take the limitations off your thinking by partnering with the Holy Spirit. We can achieve so much more because of what God has placed inside of us.

As you were made in the image of God, who creates simply by His words, meditate on how valuable your words are and how important it is to confess spiritual truth. The things you decree and declare over yourself will come to pass. It is so important that you meditate and think about God's thoughts. Let us take the limitations off our thinking by accelerating our faith in God.

John 3:34 (Amp)

> *"For He whom God has sent speaks the words of God [proclaiming the Father's own message]; for God gives the [gift of the] Spirit without measure [generously and boundlessly]!"*

MEDITATION SUPPORTS WISDOM

The temptation of incessant pre-occupation of mind is becoming increasingly rife. Sitting alone without anything in your hands to do might be scary to some, but it should be a source of joy and delight since we are never alone. Jesus is always with us and ready to interact!

Meditating as a priority on God Himself and His words means to ponder, consider, reflect, and to turn His thoughts over in your mind. So much of modern living breeds mindless living, so little time to really think and meditate.

The concept of meditation has been owned by other religions like Buddhism; so applying it to Christianity can be misunderstood. You can be meditating daily in many creative ways but intentional time should be set apart for this in order for it to become part of your subconscious mind. This is not to "empty your mind" like with other religions, but to actually fill your mind! You will know how much of the Word has penetrated your subconscious instinctive thinking when you're under pressure.

The following story illustrates how this works. A pastor from South Africa was under anesthetic for severe cancer treatment. His years of dedicated study and meditation on the Word of God had, over time, distilled from his consciousness to become part of his subconscious mind. So much so, the medical staff reported that while he was under sedation for chemotherapy he was the only patient among many who did not curse in his sleep. The wisdom of God had shone through his pain! He was quoting Scripture, preaching, or speaking in tongues!   Glory to God! There are many testimonies of how God's word has brought supernatural healing to our bodies.

It is important to note here that this form of meditation is not merely a ritual habit, but is a mind and life transforming experience based upon a *relationship* with the Author of the Bible. It has been said that the Bible is the only book that you can read while encountering the Author Himself.

Think about it! We have a power-filled, inseparable relationship with the Creator of heaven and earth through the Holy Spirit!

You can therefore instruct your mind to embrace the glory of no longer belonging to selfishness or darkness. Direct your mind to think like your Father since you are a child of God imitating your real Daddy! As He is, so can we be!

Philippians 4:8 (NKJV)

"Finally, brethren, whatever things are true, whatever things are noble, whatever things are just, whatever things are pure, whatever things are lovely, whatever things are of good report, if there is any virtue and if there is anything praiseworthy—meditate on these things

Many times I've experienced that just by merely thinking about the Lord I can physically feel His presence manifesting in my life. Before each opportunity to minister, I meditate and ponder about miracles. I think about what He's done for me and for others. I condition my mind to be flowing in His way of thinking.

PATH OF MEEKNESS

While you are divinely assisted in your quest to find greater understanding, He has placed a high regard on the attribute of meekness ~ which is the primary posture to adopt when learning more about God.

Meekness is not a word that modern society is using much, so let's look at the dictionary for the correct definition. It means: "*humbleness, submissiveness, gentleness, modesty, or being teachable*". Although Jesus came to earth as the Son of God, He chose to humble Himself as a servant (Philippians 2:7-9).

One would think that if we are being seated at the right hand of God, there is no need for meekness. But that is not so, because it is about the delegated authority given to Jesus and to us. Even though you might've walked many miles with the Lord, He always has something contrary to the world's standards to astound us with ~ and this is one of them.

The Sermon on the Mount (Matthew 5) addresses meekness as a character priority for becoming a disciple of Jesus. The word *"meekness"* in the King James Version is translated *"poor in spirit"* in the Amplified version:

Matthew 5:3 (Amp)

"Blessed [spiritually prosperous, happy, to be admired] **are the poor in spirit** [those devoid of spiritual arrogance, those who regard themselves as insignificant], **for theirs is the kingdom of heaven** [both now and forever]"

"For theirs is the kingdom of heaven." If you have been seated with Christ in heavenly places, then you know that the mindset of the heavenlies is meekness.

The astounding example Jesus gave us regarding humble kingship still challenges the most advanced intellectual. Although He was already impressive at the age of twelve in the eyes of the most learned Rabbis, and was an excellent leader by the time He called His disciples. His heart of servanthood, compassion, and love, as He matured, has become the very heart and soul of Christianity today. May our pride, arrogance, and selfishness decrease more and more as we increase in friendship with the Lord and learn to extend His right hand on earth.

Spiritual arrogance and the regard for significance of men is the breeding ground for lifeless religious ways that hold cold love and no peace. Meekness and humility is the standard by which we live devoid of ego, superiority, and pride. These are the shining godly values and ethical attitudes that produce the will of God.

Romans 12:2 (Amp)

"Do not be conformed to this world [any longer with its superficial values and customs], but be transformed and progressively changed [as you mature spiritually] by the renewing of your mind [focusing on godly values and ethical attitudes], so that you may prove [for yourselves] what the will of God is, that which is good and acceptable and perfect [in His plan and purpose for you]"

One of the vices of modern thinking is finding too much significance in things like spring cleaning our homes and detoxing our bodies, but never bothering to throw out the trash of our minds!

Honesty, integrity, and truth do not automatically come to a person with proper upbringing. These things only truly come to those who have set their minds on things above. They choose the path of righteousness.

It is therefore of vital importance that every believer knows how to apply their minds adequately ~ from carrying out menial tasks to making the most important decisions. God does not regard thinking and prayers that are not in line with His ways.

Accept today that you will increasingly be setting your mind on the Holy Spirit as the Counselor of your thought patterns (John 14:26). You will undoubtedly progress and grow in your understanding of the Lord in the meekness required. As you are given more understanding the more you'll comprehend ~ but also realize how little you know about Him.

John 14:26 (NKJV)

"But the Helper, the Holy Spirit, whom the Father will send in My name, He will teach you all things, and bring to your remembrance all things that I said to you."

ദ്ദൊ

CHAPTER 13
BUILDING THE MIND

ᎶᎹᎼ

MIND MANAGEMENT

Imagine your mind being allocated the role of an ever-mindful and considerate house **manager**, butler, or maid. The body is given the role of the **slave,** which would graciously serve the mind and the spirit. Lastly, the Spirit is allotted the role of the **mistress or master** of the household, which is the primary and most honored part of the body since it houses the glory of God.

When either good or bad thoughts come into your mind, know by the Holy Spirit, the mind of Christ, what to do with them. When positive thoughts are entertained and are allowed to "bake" in your mind-oven for victory, you inevitably become the words you speak and the reality you live in. But unfortunately the opposite is true regarding negative thoughts.

You will easily know an evil assault on your mind when you take note of the impact those thoughts have on your emotions and especially your body and digestive system.

Trust God completely to free you from anything like selfishness, lust, or worldly desires ~ as those destructive and unchecked thoughts seek out areas in your life to attach themselves to you. Many who have neglected taking their thoughts captive have reported a decline in health, so this is worth taking seriously!

Luke 10:19 (Amp)

"Listen carefully: I have given you authority [that you now possess] to tread on serpents and scorpions, and [the ability to exercise authority] over all the power of the enemy (Satan); and nothing will [in any way] harm you"

Think of words contrary to God's thoughts as the "serpents" and the "scorpions" that Jesus has given you power to trample upon. You have authority over them (Luke 10:19)! For if the bad thoughts are not allowed to be "baked" and you refuse to entertain them to full fruition, they will have absolutely no effect on you and you will continue walking in the path of life. We cannot stop the proverbial birds from flying over our heads, but we can stop them from building a nest in our hair!

James 1:13-16 (Amp)

"But each one is tempted when he is dragged away, enticed and baited [to commit sin] by his own [worldly] desire (lust, passion). Then when the illicit desire has conceived, it gives birth to sin; and when sin has run its course, it gives birth to death. Do not be misled, my beloved brothers and sisters"

THE MIND'S DOORKEEPER

Great people have great thoughts. I've never met a small-minded person who is significant and has achieved great things. Though great-minded people are generally quite humble and realistic about themselves, there is a deep-seated knowing that they are able to achieve anything they put their minds to.

The mind is a door of life and you are its only doorkeeper, because there is something God wants to achieve through this "portal". Satan cannot penetrate or even control your mind. He can only make an attempt at projecting evil thoughts, and distracting you by influence or negativity. Just like light dispels darkness, see your mind as a weapon of light that eliminates any dark negative words and actions. Always believe you are the ultimate best and you are divinely unique. As you take care of yourself, you'll take care of others.

When God created you He made you unique. Start meditating on your exceptional greatness through His power (Ephesians 1:19). Stay inspired by the success stories of faith heroes (Hebrews 11), as the opportunities arise, start asking questions from those who have come into significance. Remember, your motive is to help yourself so you can benefit others.

Quit thinking about what you can't do and start developing a can-do attitude by that peaceful knowing that you have the wisdom and solutions of Christ. Confidence will develop through this optimistic, God-led thinking. Get to know what God has put in you and allow Him to grow and mature in those things.

You will begin to distinctly profit from this financially, and have the tenacity that accelerates you past mere achievements and success and brings you into significance and purpose.

THE BLUEPRINT OF HIS WORD

What your focus is on is what you will become. The Word of God is like that blueprint architects use to refer to in the building process. It is my prayer that you start focusing on things that are worth spending your time on, and to keep building your life on the thoughts of God. Meditate upon the true, noble, and things of good report as the Scripture instructs.

Matthew 7:24 (NKJV)

"Therefore whoever hears these sayings of Mine, and does them, I will liken him to a wise man who built his house on the rock"

We see negativity everywhere ~ in media and through conversations all around us as the fallen nature gets preyed on through the demonic. Design a heavenly picture of good things and focus on the heavenly.

When you find yourself in a difficult situation, start visualizing the ideal ~ what God has built on the Rock of Christ. For instance, if you are stuck in poverty, start imagining what your heavenly home looks like, what your environment, should look like. Imagine the joy and the peace you will be experiencing in that environment and the effect it will have on your sense of well-being. By visualizing the love and beauty God has prepared for you, you will erupt in worship and praise, with a skip and a joy in your step. Refuse to go into the negative and to allow your mind to control your emotions and your will.

In my first book, *You Shall Live,* I wrote about my difficult childhood and the challenging circumstances I was exposed to. These circumstances are now my testimony of how God can transform someone from poverty to prosperity. If God had not given me a blueprint of Himself and how He sees me, I would not have been able to come out of that way of thinking.

During that time I also saw how negative thinking could keep people in sinful lifestyles.

It is important to stick to the blueprint of God's Word for it will most definitely receive opposition. Ministers who criticize other ministries that are wealthy are hardly ever wealthy themselves. This proves there is a lack of revelation of the intention of the Lord. Those who are walking in abundance will testify that wealth has never just "dropped from the sky". God normally works with the heart before He fills the baskets, and that is a process of spiritual and character maturity.

Christian businesspersons have also testified that receiving finance, whether little or much, is a territory to be handled with great dependence and trust in the Lord. For an abundant bank account also serves to refine the heart. With great wealth comes great responsibility, and not everyone has the constitution or maturity to handle God's riches with godly stewardship. Many want to be wealthy but very few are willing to have the grit to cooperate with God by sticking to His plan.

The Holy Spirit teaches shrewd business practice and provides riches and wealth, not just for our well-being but to keep our hearts in the right place and to extend His purposes.

If you do not regard money as your servant for His kingdom, it will eventually lead you back to the orphan spirit, which leads to poverty. Fruitlessness and financial squandering will result.

Choose to be free from the superficial pleasures of riches that choke the promises of God, but break free into hearing and doing the word of God through a generous spirit. Seek His kingdom first ~ find out where the mature kingdom orchards are and invest your time and talents there to start becoming fruitful. God will provide the treasure if your greatest treasure lies in the heavenlies.

Luke 11:13 (Amp)

"If you, then, being evil [that is, sinful by nature], know how to give good gifts to your children, how much more will your heavenly Father give the Holy Spirit to those who ask and continue to ask Him!"

DON'T REBUILD THE PAST

Everyone makes mistakes and no one is immune to them ~ it is part of what we face as humans. Sometimes a scar from the past is so painful that we can get stuck in that memory, building our future on that one incident. Some even build their identities from that one reference, allowing it to define them.

Instead of living in the past, shift your focus. Look at your life through the eyes of Jesus. You need to define what the cross personally means to you ~ His sacrifice washing you with His blood and giving you a new name. Jesus called this experience being "born again" when He spoke to Cornelius in John 3 ~ this is the epitome of having presence of mind.

By simply and humbly accepting this grace by faith right now, He will start building an identity in you that cannot be broken down ~ it is permanent and eternal. This is the infallible identity of Christ ~ your Rock that is immovable.

By choosing this presence of mind (I cannot help but notice the play of words with "presents"). You choose to focus on His presence ~ knowing Him and not being distracted by being hung up by insecurities, faults, or mistakes. The great thing about it is that most people don't really care about your struggles. What they do take note of is obvious victories over them. As you focus on what Jesus has done and not the sin you have committed, you will find you will become less concerned with your humanity and more sensitive about returning your love to Him. That also means not grieving Him, and having remorse even for the smallest mistake, because His love eclipses your identity.

There are those who religiously watch something happen, and then there are those who actually seize the moment. They get their hands dirty by getting involved with things that move the heart of God. In contradiction to the popular song lyric, *"From A Distance"*; He is most definitely not an indifferent bystander! Many choose to only observe His kingdom from a distant and impersonal place because of all kinds of excuses and unbelief, and don't allow their lives be defined by what Jesus accomplished.

This means heeding to the initiative warnings He gives, humbly allowing and enduring the discomfort of breaking down self-accomplishment. It trusts Him to build His true character and unshakeable kingdom in you that endures through any pain, disaster, or disease.

Hebrews 12:27-29 (MSG)

"So don't turn a deaf ear to these gracious words. If those who ignored earthly warnings didn't get away with it, what will happen to us if we turn our backs on heavenly warnings? His voice that time shook the earth to its foundations; this time—He's told us this quite plainly—He'll also rock the heavens: 'One last shaking, from top to bottom, stem to stern.' The phrase 'one last shaking' means a thorough housecleaning, getting rid of all the historical and religious junk so that the unshakable essentials stand clear and uncluttered.

Do you see what we've got? An unshakable kingdom! And do you see how thankful we must be? Not only thankful, but brimming with worship, deeply reverent before God. For God is not an indifferent bystander. He's actively cleaning house, torching all that needs to burn, and he won't quit until it's all cleansed. God himself is Fire!"

SOLID WALLS

Just like the enemy wanted to prohibit Nehemiah from rebuilding the wall of Jerusalem, so the enemy today wants people blinded to the mind of Christ to bring restoration of mind. He is using an array of tactics to place the focus on either our own shortcomings or those of others. Know that once you are building your life upon the mind of Christ, it, like the quality of bricks, will be tested.

Just like a building is built one brick at a time, so thoughts can build a mindset or an attitude. It is an interesting comparison, that like the word of God is refined seven times, so Civil Engineers have a seven-point quality test-to-test bricks.

Psalm 12:6

"The words of the Lord are pure words, like silver tried in a furnace of earth, purified seven times"

The firing of bricks is the fourth and last level of manufacturing quality bricks. Applying the mind of Christ is a process Christ leads us to. Our thoughts become purified from all foreign matter, lasting through the seven tests, which bring about true renewed thinking. When we worship in spirit and truth, we allow the fiery presence of God to purify our thinking. The fire of the Word of God not only burns all the impurities of our humanity, but His love purifies us to the degree likened unto refined gold.

It is no wonder that the streets of the new heavenly Jerusalem are made of gold. This may be to remind us of the path we followed to renewed thinking. The foundational layers are made of the gemstones of the priestly breastplate, jewels that are also formed from

May you embrace the processes of the heavenly building in your life. John the Baptist introduced disciples to changed behavior by water baptism, but Jesus the Baptizer introduced us to changed hearts by baptism of fire. This is the new covenant of righteousness we now live in by the renewal of heart and mind.

Revelation 3:18 (Amp)

"I counsel you to buy from Me gold that has been heated red hot and refined by fire so that you may become truly rich; and white clothes [representing righteousness] to clothe yourself so that the shame of your nakedness will not be seen; and healing salve to put on your eyes so that you may see"

The so-called Christians, who look polished from the outside but choose to remain untouched by the passion and fire of God on the inside, are those who are a misrepresentation of the faith. For those only glancing at faith because of the fear of change, will never progress towards that fulfillment that only the pure love of God can give.

John the Revelator sees Christ the conqueror as one with eyes like flames of fire:

Revelation 19:11-13 (Amp)

"And I saw heaven opened, and behold, a white horse, and He who was riding it is called Faithful and True (trustworthy, loyal, incorruptible, steady), and in righteousness He judges and wages war [on the rebellious nations].

His eyes are a flame of fire, and on His head are many royal crowns; and He has a name inscribed [on Him] which no one knows or understands except Himself. He is dressed in a robe dipped in blood, and His name is called The Word of God."

When you are experiencing a refining and a testing, you are in the baptism of fire with the Lord. You are in the process of building those tested and tried solid bricks of the foundation of Christ in your life. But remember, He is *with* you in this intimate molding and building process. As Daniel and his friends had presence of mind within the smoldering flames of the Babylonians, so the Holy Spirit's flame in your heart will keep you from anything that will harm you.

Hebrews 12:28 (AMP)

"Therefore, since we receive a kingdom which cannot be shaken, let us show gratitude, and offer to God pleasing service and acceptable worship with reverence and awe."

CRUD

222

CHAPTER 14
GUARDING THE MIND

ଔଓ

John 1:4-5 (NKJV)

"In Him was life and the life was the light of men. And the light shines in the darkness, and the darkness did not comprehend it"

STEALTH-LIGHT OF MIND

The mind of Christ illuminates your natural mind and will always cause you to outshine every obstacle, test, or dark attempt on your life. His mind in your intellect, will, and emotions are made to seize victory, lay hold on His promises and overcome darkness ~ including every problem or negative way of thinking.

The mind of Christ is the guard to the "gateway to heavenly thinking" that overcomes the darkness of natural, even demonic thinking. An unrenewed or uncommitted mind is thus an unguarded mind that becomes a "gateway to hell. The word *"comprehend"* in John 1:5 is *"katalambano"* in the Greek, which is also interpreted, *"to seize, lay hold of, and overcome"*.

True comprehension by the mind of Christ is therefore an ability to both submit to God, and to have a "handle on life" so to speak. It is an inner confidence of who God is, who you are, and how that translates to a life of exciting and abundant living. Even in grave challenges, the ability to figure out what to do and how to press into it is granted, provided that we live as if we have already received the ideal. Paul knew that he could not really reach perfection in this life, but his goal was to "press on" as if it were attainable.

Philippians 3:12 (AMP)

"Not that I have already obtained it [this goal of being Christ-like] or have already been made perfect, but I actively press on so that I may take hold of that [perfection] for which Christ Jesus took hold of me and made me His own"

My encounter with a Satanist on assignment in Zambia illustrates how this "handle on life" protects and guides us. After my car broke down on the way to a prayer meeting one day, I sat disturbed and disappointed in the waiting room of the repair shop. Being grateful for surviving a potential life-threatening situation, as the Lord would have it I was obliviously seated right next to the Satanist who had been trying to deter me! In an uncomfortable introduction of small talk, the man revealed his evil intention quite soon, claiming he instigated my car's breakdown. He found satisfaction in the fact that I could not attend the prayer meeting.

With every nerve on edge and senses reeling, I became astutely aware of how unprepared I was for this confrontation. Despite the intention of preparing myself spiritually for the prayer meeting, I was totally caught off-guard while I was on the *way* to prayer. It dawned on me that the prayer meeting was meant to start right there so I began to pray in the Spirit. Usually when I engage in prayer in this manner my senses sharpen, and sometimes God even grants me discernment. Without me knowing it, I was agreeing with God for this man's spiritual sight to open up. Suddenly he started shouting while covering his eyes! Just like at Paul's conversion, he was able to see a bright light but I could not. God had provided me an angel of light to protect and guard me.

With some discretion to not cause too much a public commotion, I reasoned with the man that if he let go of the evil spirit and received the Lord Jesus, I would pray that the angel would be commissioned to guard him from any of the demons to come back again. He promptly agreed and he was delivered of the evil spirit!

The light of God does not only shine a path for you, but it also dispels darkness invading your environment. Being connected with the

Holy Spirit as your closest companion, friend, and counselor brings you to spiritual awareness for the benefit of your situation and that of others. Remember, you have an understanding and knowing that cannot be grasped by a darkened mind.

You, however, will have *discernment* into other minds, even the mind of the enemy and know how to apply wisdom in each circumstance!

John 2:24 (Amp)

"But Jesus, for His part, did not entrust Himself to them, because He knew all **people** *[and understood the superficiality and fickleness of human nature]"*

As Jesus fully knew and understood human nature, allow His mind to minister this understanding to you. At times we waste so much time trying to explain why God hates sin or how the gifts of the Holy Spirit work, when people are veiled by a darkened mind.

As Moses came down from the mountain in Exodus 34:29-35, having received the law for the second time on tablets of stone, he was unaware that his *face* was shining from having been with God. When Jesus was transfigured on the mount in Matthew 17, His *whole body* shone with the glory of God. I believe that the illumination of our hearts and minds in Christ can bring physical manifestations that bring back the awe and fear of God in our spirits, souls and bodies. The fear of the Lord needs to return to the nations of the world by the radiance of the Lord emanating from our faces and bodies. We are in desperate need for His manifest glory operating through His body.

The evidence of the Lord's involvement and love for our planet is growing exponentially through His people.

Studies of the universe and of archaeological findings show that God's ways and the Bible are proven to be scientifically correct. However, being correct is not the purpose of learning to think like the Lord. It is merely accepting by *faith* what God already has provided for our benefit ~ a mind patterned after God's life-giving ways. We are to simply embrace and unswervingly trust the mind of the Holy Spirit.

WARRIOR OF TRUTH

Many believers have a partial truth about the nature of God. Part of renewing your mind to think like God is to understand that He not only is a Lover and a Father but He is also a warrior and we are to identify ourselves as such. We have the gentleness of a shepherd friend and Father, *and* the ferocity of the Lion of Judah whenever needed.

In 2010 I felt doomed and my life was not going anywhere. To make matters worse, my health was suffering and the doctor told me I might die. All my dreams of working for the

Lord and traveling the world were still in my heart, but my mind was not cooperating! I felt tempted to heed to the sentence of the doctor until the Lord spoke to me and said, *"You shall live!"* From that point on my mind was reactivated and soon afterward, overcoming action resulted. The warrior spirit of the Lord had kicked in!

I even used the whole experience of God's restoration as a means to author my first book, "You Shall Live!"

Even greater creativity came after the book was written, for the voice of the Lord is the source of all creativity. I started shaping the words from my book into lyrics for revelatory songs about the Lord and His kingdom. As we even progressed to recording the songs, I was singing the songs of the Lord given to me back to Him, building my confidence and faith in the Lord even more!

Looking back, I realized God was leading me to operate in the mind of the warrior, as is found in the account of Jehoshaphat's army, who won the battle by another's means.

2 Chronicles 20:17 (NKJ)

"You will need to fight in this battle. Position yourselves, stand still and see the salvation of the Lord, who is with you, O Judah and Jerusalem! Do not fear or be dismayed; tomorrow go out against them, for the Lord is with you"

I realized through the battle of my health, that my spiritual eyes had been opened and I could gradually dream and visualize again! Dreams can be shattered by disappointments, but if you will just seek and heed that one word from the Lord, it will catapult you into expanding dimensions of His glorious hope! His song of victory came forth because I had cooperated with Him.

2 Chronicles 20:21-22 (NKJ)

"And when he had consulted with the people, he appointed those who should sing to the Lord, and who should praise the beauty of holiness, as they went out before the army and were saying: 'Praise the Lord, For His mercy endures forever.' Now when they began to sing and to praise, the Lord set ambushes against the people of Ammon, Moab and Mount Sier, who had come against Judah, and they were defeated"

Some of you may be going through such challenging issues, that it could be affecting your attitude and faith to advance. You might be at a point that you know your business or ministry has to expand, but you don't know how to take that next step. Right now you need to stop everything that's keeping you busy, and calm your mind and your thoughts. Prepare to receive the Word of the Lord and His gentle voice whispering to you. Shut everything off and posture yourself to humbly worship, listen, and learn from Him.

Inspire your thinking concerning the warrior attitude of the Lord Jesus. The spirit of praise will start overtaking your thoughts as you realize that the Lord has already broken into the heavenlies for you ~ to open the gates of praise and shut the gates of the enemy advancing against you.

Take on His persistent, tenacious attitude. Even if it seems God is silent, not hearing from God is not that God refuses to speak, but your spiritual senses could be clogged by ignorance or disobedience. You could also have issues that need to be dealt with, and unforgiveness that needs to be confessed. The Holy Spirit is faithful to reveal these hindrances to your heart and God is always all about communication! Just like any good army has an intelligence department to feed information and communication, so the Lord is equipping you for battle.

TRANSPARENCY

In September 2015, I was ministering at a church when a powerful manifestation of the glory of God appeared in the building. A man testified that during these sessions he was healed of painful chronic ear infections. He tells that as soon as I laid my hands on this man he just knew by the Holy Spirit that he was touched and healed. The ear infection was permanently banned from his body! I recognized that as he was testifying in front of the church, which I'm sure took a lot of courage to do as it was not comfortable for him. I recognized such a glory of God manifesting in the atmosphere as he spoke. As I took his hand after the testimony we started worshipping Jesus and so many more people were healed!

Sometimes part of the battle is just being honest with the Lord. David was a man after God's heart who openly confessed his weaknesses to the Lord, even the feeling of being overwhelmed. But as soon as he did He was able to realize he had a defense! He was able see the Lord as that Rock that was higher than his circumstance, higher than his emotions, and higher than his weaknesses and sin.

Psalm 61:2 (Amp)

"From the end of the earth I call to You, when my heart is overwhelmed and weak; lead me to the rock that is higher than I [a rock that is too high to reach without Your help]"

Once your conscience is clear, start meditating on all the times He has empowered and helped you to be a success in the past. Start thanking Him for all the times you've called to Him and He has answered and helped you. You might even be prompted to remember things you haven't yet thanked Him for, or even realized

He had been with you. This is simply getting your mind channeled into thinking in the way that God thinks about you. As you continue, soon your mind will be set on a course that the Holy Spirit will take you ~ giving you insight into the present and also plans for the future.

The temptation of Christ in Luke 4 reveals how Jesus was trained to acquire this attribute of warrior-like honesty and godliness.

Having His thoughts armed, the words of Jesus was a both a weapon of defense and of attack against Satan. Meditating upon the truth of the Word of God and wielding it in times of temptation, is your "under cover weapon" from heaven! The mind of Christ in you is a stealth weapon against the enemy. You only need to submit and learn to use it well.

Being obedient to His word is operating in His mind of hidden truth. It cannot be discerned by darkened minds and always shines brighter and breaks through every temptation, test, or trail.

It is thus imperative for successful living to understand His mind (standard), so that we posture ourselves appropriately in worship and in our relationship with God. We need not be anxious about the tactics of Satan, for the Lord has already overcome him! The mind of Christ has overcome!

THOUGHTS OF VALOUR

I encourage you to find Spirit-filled warriors to associate with. They are the ones who go before the battle of the Lord with the weapons of high praise and worship.

Scripture reveals in Judges 6 that Gideon was in the place of small-minded thinking before he was supernaturally called by the Lord to lead His battle.

Just like Gideon, we allow fear to either paralyze us, or keep us too busy so that we either forget or neglect to know who God has formed us and called us for.

We learn from the story of Gideon that despite his low opinion of himself the angel addressed him according to his heavenly persona, which was "mighty man of valor" (Judges 6:12). It is by this title and anointing that God continued to deal with, and address Gideon. What makes you therefore any different? If you continue to be small in your own eyes while the Word of God declares that you are great in God's eyes, you will continue in mediocre thinking bringing about no advancement in your life. God wants to extend His joyful grace to you in providing you His identity to overcome any lack or poverty. In the midst of this great race of faith, which has its hills and valleys, is the focus on your greatest wealth ~ your name being written in the Lamb's book of life (Luke 10:20)?

The sacrifice of Jesus has redeemed you and has bought you eternal access to God's goodness and glory. The open door to heaven's recesses, is allowing God to be renewing your natural mind to think like royalty. This one singular act of God should be the source of great joy and thankfulness spilling over our hearts and through lips each morning.

Your mind is your gold mine from which you live out your royal persona bought by the blood of Jesus.

The only limitations of your mind are those thoughts you yourself have created, those mindsets where you have allowed circumstances, or the opinions of others, to define you.

This rebirth by faith is the most powerful force that has emancipated you from prison and pauper-like thinking. Once you break this cycle of negative or dark thinking by the illumination of God's Word, you break through to a glorious realm of perfect joy and love ~ of yourself and of others. You no longer have a selfish mediocre way of living, that breaths relief from merely surviving. You are able to anticipate the deep breaths of God's rhythms of grace that sustain you into great fruitfulness and prosperity in every area of life. Your life becomes a picture of the advanced work of the cross.

For too long the image of the church has been limited to the function of helping people achieve their personal goals. They have been preparing spiritual "food parcels" for needy people, instead of teaching them to "have dominion" as God declared over Adam. God has planted in each individual the desire to go beyond this beggar mentality to make the world a better place. God has equipped us to take our place as a unique part that will bring life, joy, and support to the body ~ and even fund the church and to send missionaries. Our cooperation and partnership with the Holy Spirit is the source of great advancement of the kingdom of God, not just for our own benefit.

PROTECT YOUR MIND

Prohibit yourself watching and listening to material that will negatively effect the positive environment you envision to grow. Things that bring you down or remind you of your past failures, do not contribute to the development of the mind of Christ.

Release your past and let "bygones be bygones". You can do nothing about what has already transpired, but you can transform those anxieties to praise. Begin to encourage yourself that even in your losses, there is hope that God is more than able to restore your life, relationships, and gift you with physical rewards. He is a God of improvement, He is the God of "the better", as is discussed in the book of Hebrews ~ a better covenant, an improved reality, and a greater future!

As much as we want to control people, they have their own minds and, mostly a strong will. These aspects need not control you. We generally cannot control other people but we can direct the environment we create for ourselves. What you have in your environment is what you have allowed, and so creating positivity and faith to be part of your environment can only nurture and strengthen you and everyone else you encounter.

You cannot afford to allow anybody or anything to influence or manipulate you out of that sphere that God has granted you in Christ.

You are the one that is to stand like that immoveable lighthouse, the one being the gracious influencer in *their* lives. Jesus said He will build His church on Himself ~ the immoveable Rock of revelation (Matt.16:14-16). We strengthen ourselves this way, and protect our minds by adopting *His* mind about life.

It doesn't help if you are only able to quote Scripture, but you know nothing about obeying it. A head full of knowledge doesn't necessarily *enable* you to understand and do the principles of the Word. Let your personal revelation of Christ not only remain a prayer, but let it become a reality in your daily living. As Jesus is the incarnate Word of God, you are to determine that the principles of the Word should be in *both* your walk and talk. You are protecting your mind by becoming the Word.

Since your emotions are inside your mind, the mind of Christ redeems your emotions. Your personality is gradually manifesting by Christ's life-giving spirit in you. This is a great advantage in attracting people to you, and you will find you have great likeability because of this. This only is so you will draw people to Christ and His truth, and not due to anything yourself. Your attractiveness is thus in Christ, and this is true and healthy self-esteem.

Luke 6:38 (NKJV)
"Give, and it will be given to you. Good measure, pressed down, shaken together, running over, will be put into your lap. For with the measure you use it will be measured back to you"

The principles you uphold, and the integral manner in which you do things, attracts people to you. Understand that you are receiving this ability by the wisdom of God. His wisdom makes you win, exceed, and excel ~ it is that supernatural zone that gives you the vantage point in life. That is why the enemy's strategies are to undervalue the Word of God, for therein lies your victory.

GUARDING BY LOVE AND PEACE

The mind of Christ within is not only meant to be understood, but nurtured. The development of Godly thinking is taken care of by building the guard of a positive environment. Wherever there is weakness, stubborn, sin, or brokenness, you can be sure the delay towards transformation rests mainly on spiritual ignorance and malnutrition. Since the mind of Christ has the inherent ability to create supernaturally, it is your personal prerogative to *create* this positive environment through love, in order for your mind to be protected and to grow.

As a saint who has access to all heavenly resources, you do not have the liberty to justify the ineffective environment you have allowed. Things like poor decisions in the past, low economic standing, educational disadvantage, or circumstantial pressures ~ are all part of a temporal environment. Your permanent position is the wisdom of love.

The wisdom of Christ allows you to see past the limitations and accusations of selfishness and to lovingly nurture your environment for the right reasons. A growing mind in Christ harbors the pure motives of investing in self-growth, to be enabled to help others grow. In the Scripture below, we see that loving yourself is part of the commitment to love the Lord.

Matthew 22: 35-40 (Amp)

"One of them, a lawyer [an expert in Mosaic Law], asked Jesus a question, to test Him: 'Teacher, which is the greatest commandment in the Law?' And Jesus replied to him, 'YOU SHALL LOVE THE LORD YOUR GOD WITH ALL YOUR HEART, AND WITH ALL YOUR SOUL, AND WITH ALL YOUR MIND.

This is the first and greatest commandment. The second is like it, YOU SHALL LOVE YOUR NEIGHBOR AS YOURSELF [that is, unselfishly seek the best or higher good for others]. The whole Law and the [writings of the] Prophets depend on these two commandments.'"

After filling your life with loving God first, fill your life with loving, godly, wise, and positive people who recognize Christ in you. These are those who discern the character and destiny Christ has made you to become. They are willing to support and help you build your courage, no matter what your present or past. They see prophetically the transforming power of Christ demonstrating His sacrificial love to you.

Sometimes it's hard to find such people ~ even complicated! You can implore the Lord's help and He will supply the supernatural means to recognize and utilize the relationships He brings your way. Do not listen to just everybody, or blindly welcome everyone, but be specific in your request to the Lord concerning which attributes in your character need strengthening and courage. In this way you will recognize the Lord answering you.

In addition to building Godly relationships, keep a lookout for Holy Spirit inspired books and videos that will encourage and nourish you. Make sure that the resources you choose are encouraging you to love and to do good, feeding your courage and strengthening your weaknesses. Once again, do not just watch anything, or everything, but make sure that what you engage in will mature you.

Know yourself through others. Relationships build our character. So if, for example, people are constantly offending you, you need to know *what* is triggering you. A natural reaction is *"Is it me or is it them?"* Ultimately, your mind in Christ should be unoffendable, for what God created you to be is generally not the normal mindset in others. Therefore, stay in meditation of His Word in your mind.

Once again, the Holy Spirit is your Helper to discern these things. If your mind is at rest in the Word, your discernment is sharper and more prompt. You will be able to adequately respond to such behavior. As you cannot continue living your life avoiding all conflict and difficult situations, sometimes you need to pick your battles. You need to know *how* to engage, and when to let things be.

In addition to peace, staying in love with the Lord will keep you walking in the Spirit, and He will help you communicate well. This love endures and overcomes all contradictions ~ with wisdom, dignity and composure (1 Cor. 13:7).

All you need to do is to be available and obedient to the Lord. Signs and miracles following your prayers and ministry is your rightful inheritance in Jesus!

CBEO

CHAPTER 15
MIND COMBAT

ೞೲ

THE WARRIOR COACH

A friend once told me of a vision she had while in intercession and prayer over a very difficult circumstance in her life. The only thing she knew to do was to hit the floor weeping before the Lord in frustration and anxiety. Through tears she imagined what Jesus would've done in this situation, and so was transported in the Spirit to a vision of Jesus praying in the garden.

At first, it looked like He was bent over on one knee in intercession. But upon coming closer she realized He held a surprising expression. It seemed like He was mimicking her posture of grief, but He was actually coming aside her like a weight-trainer would do at the gym. He was edging her on from a groan from deep inside Him ~ He had perfect empathy and association for her deepest hurts and emotions, but was not coddling her comfort in self-pity.

She suddenly saw Jesus in another light ~ the Warrior Coach!

When the heavy weights of life are being pushed upon you and your muscles seem to want to snap, when you are bearing down to birth the dreams of the Lord in your life, think of the All-powerful Jesus strengthening and cheering you on with His unstoppable love. He has borne much more and much further for you than you can ever imagine!

Sometimes we just need to receive, not only the comfort of the Lord, but His tenacious grit to endure, to depend on His strength to see us through. The Lord is in all things, and wanting to be part of everything in our lives ~ both the great and the small, the seemingly impossible to the easier things. Make Him that full covenant partner that you so desire.

A MIND FOR BATTLE

The light of Christ within opposes and dispels all forms of darkness (John 1:5), and so having a circumspect approach in our daily walk is something each of have to commit to and expect to engage in. When John baptized Jesus, the Holy Spirit was manifested. That marked the start of His ministry as an example to us. His first assignment was a battle with Satan in the wilderness. Many of us need to come out of our comfort thinking that the Holy Spirit is mainly there for our comfort, but also for our aid to combat darkness.

Christians with non-confrontational personalities really need to come out of the excuse of not being naturally combative, by renewing their thinking about their identity in Christ. It is these very ones that the enemy is targeting and so a change in mindset will bring great victories.

In the letter to the Ephesians the Apostle Paul used five chapters to instruct and teach the church, especially concerning their identity in Christ. But we have to ask ourselves the question, to what end? The sixth and final chapter reveals that we are equipped for one purpose, and that is for battle in prayer so that our conduct and practice brings about the kingdom and power of God.

Many Christians do not have an awareness of the intensity and seriousness of the battle for our souls, since they have taken an attitude that battling the enemy is primarily something the Lord does. Once again, the word of God sheds light on our attitude and approach to become trained and ready for combat in cooperation with heaven. The Lord does not need us to enforce His kingdom, He only needs our cooperation in choosing us to partner in His victory through Christ.

Realize that you have been chosen to experience His amazing grace and kindness in giving you everything you need for life and godliness (2 Peter 1:3). Even though He is the source of all power and authority, He chooses to use us with Christ, as His kingdom representatives to dispel the darkness.

All great battles faced in life start in the mind, and therefore the greatest victories forged all originated in the mind. The Message translation concludes this in such an inspirational way:

Ephesians 6:10-12 (The Message)

"And that about wraps it up. God is strong, and He wants you strong. So take everything the Master has set out for you, well-made weapons of the best materials. And put them to use so you will be able to stand up to everything the Devil throws your way. This is no afternoon athletic contest that we'll walk away from and forget about in a couple of hours. This is for keeps, a life-or-death fight to the finish against the Devil and all his angels."

BATTLE OF THE MIND

A study on how spiritual warfare works is in the account of Joseph, who received strategies in a dream from the Lord to avoid the murderous plots of Herod to kill the baby Jesus (Matthew 2:13-15).

Be aware that when the Lord grants you a dream, vision, or prophetic word ~ it is a weapon of warfare to be wielded for your advantage and empowerment. This is a responsible response to the information God is giving to you from heaven.

In 2014, I met a woman at a farewell party. She said she was totally changed through prophetic words God gave me for her at one of our meetings. She shared how God changed her life after that night. The right word from God at the right moment can completely transform your life. God can also use you as a mighty prophetic instrument in His hand to bring purpose and direction to the lives of His people.

There are so many more many examples in the Old Testament ~ characters like David, Gideon and Jehoshaphat ~ who received overcoming power by God's direct intervention through their attributes of spiritual vision. You have access to the mind of Christ!

COMBAT BAD HABITS

How do we break destructive addictions, bad habits, and other hang-ups? It's all about taking note how they developed in the first place ~ over time; throughout all that time your soul and your spirit were being malnourished and dehydrated. No wonder there is little moral strength, strength of character, the ability to say no among so many!

As our spirits and bodies mature our minds must also grow. You are today who you have daily formed in your mind over time, and that includes what your parents, relatives, and friends have confessed over you.

Sometimes, DNA transfers disease or inabilities, but most of the time people allow sickness and disease to take hold of their minds and bodies.

It's interesting to note how disease is related to certain addictions that can only be broken by the anointing and dealing with another disease first. We need the mind and wisdom of God to apply in situations that do not make sense.

Years ago I was ministering in Carson, California, speaking with Reverend Mar. In the meeting a woman was miraculously healed from blindness! Where she once could not see, she suddenly could see perfectly! Not only did the Lord do this for her, but He also touched and delivered her from an addiction to sugar. He cares about those things too! Another woman was delivered from an anger problem. As we can all probably relate, no child of God should be riddled with bad habits ~ and He is ready to deliver us from these things if we allow Him.

If you have allowed it certain circumstances have also formed the way you think of yourself. In addition the way you see yourself in the world you have created by allowing influences by observing certain images, models, examples, listening and learning information. Over time these things have formed your identity and persona.

You need to accept the fact that just as it took time to form your habits, it will also take you committing to daily time in the Word and prayer to renew your thinking.

Insecurities play another part.

Sometimes you find yourself in a company of people who do not like you. For most people, the natural reaction is to feel rejection, self-doubt, and a pre-occupation of all the reasons why you are not being accepted. At such a time, provided that you have not willfully offended or stepped out of loving them or caused unnecessary attention to yourself, purposefully combat negative thoughts with the mind of Christ.

Don't allow yourself to develop low self-esteem as you identify an attack on the mind of Christ within you. Firstly, you need to not become self-defensive, but take hold of your mind processes and start visualizing how God has created you in His image ~ your spirit, soul, and body created perfectly (review chapter 2).

See yourself chosen of God at this time, and return to the joy and the privilege of being alive. Learn to activate the positive energy of the Holy Spirit and He will restore that perfect identity and joy of self-worth.

The Bible declares that as a person thinks, so shall he or she be (Proverbs 23:7). Resist the development of thinking reactively, and shift your focus on thinking intuitively to that inner *knowing.* Allow the Holy Spirit to enhance the truth of His thoughts towards you. These thoughts of truth will set you free from the bondage you are habitually forming within your mind.

John 8:31-32 (NKJ)

"Then Jesus said to those Jews who believed Him, 'If you abide in My word, you are My disciples indeed. And you shall know the truth, and the truth shall make you free'"

AN OVERCOMING MIND

Since Christ has overcome the world, we continue that overcoming victory in our daily living by the Holy Spirit's provision. He has granted us much daily protection, courage, and bravery in this lost and decaying world.

No matter what the world throws at us, we have perfect peace in knowing He has provided and He has overcome. Only God could think up something, like peace, being a weapon!

We are therefore completely equipped, empowered, and enabled to overcome. Be sheltered and strengthened while living out His call in this world.

This peace, however, does not position us in a complacent, corner-hugging posture, waiting for rapture-day. But it enables a brave and prompt availability to the Lord ~ being at His command, engaging in His battle, and enforcing His kingdom purposes. In the end we win, but we win *today* in every way! There are no failures or orphans in the kingdom of God and there are also no achievements or wins without His glory.

In the process of renewing your mind in Christ, you are consistently engaging in a battle, not of your circumstances, but of your thoughts. This is not denying the likes of terrorists, tsunamis, or torture. But accepting part of your identity as a child of God, is accepting that you have also been offered to adopt the warrior-spirit of Jesus as the overcoming Christ within.

Accept the invitation right now into His accomplished victory, which He battled for you in prayer in the Garden of Gethsemane. He is the Overcomer in you who completely finished the fight of sin on your behalf on the cross of Calvary. His resurrection power within is your life-coach and your trainer for overcoming victory through His word.

UNSHAKEABLE MINDSET

By receiving this tremendous power and incredible identity, you are also receiving His unshakeable kingdom, which is in direct opposition to anything that is anti-Christ. By the Word of God your mind is equipped to identify, and discern what is in opposition to your identity and your God-given assignment. His Spirit knows how to reinforce this identity and provide you the subsequent acting responsibility as a true Spirit-filled representative of Jesus.

As Christ is, so are we in this world (2 Corinthians 10:7). So although we portray the attitude of meekness, servanthood, humbleness, gentleness, and love as the Lamb who was slain, we are also intolerant and proactive against temptations and demonic attacks, like the conquering Lion of Judah. Posture yourself daily before the Lord, allow Him to train you and to use you to enforce His will and His kingdom to transform your environment.

I've heard of Christians experiencing reoccurring and traumatic circumstances in their lives, and that is when that Warrior-Spirit of the Lord needs to be called back. We also need to prayerfully investigate His Word and use our inner intuition as to why these things are happening. As you rest and soak in His unchangeable Person, He will show you clearly where you are allowing spiritual breaches to occur, and what He is coaching you to do in the areas where your mind still needs renewing.

RENEWED THROUGH TESTING

So, with the mindset of a glorious servant-soldier-in-training unto the Most High God, *"be transformed by the renewing of your mind and so prove what the will of God is"* (Romans 12:1). Welcome the process, His will, but also be comforted in identifying when He is testing your character.

This is not to punish or harshly discipline you without cause. This is so you are enabled to use your spiritual weapons with heavenly wisdom. Regard the trails and temptations as instruments of God's grace to bring you to a place of becoming a mature warrior in the Lord, wielding the highest weaponry of the Spirit with accuracy and integrity.

2 Timothy 2:15 (Amp)

"Study and do your best to present yourself to God approved, a workman [tested by trial] who has no reason to be ashamed, accurately handling and skillfully teaching the word of truth"

He is, after all, coming not only for a conquering Bride but also for pure and spotless ones who is able to teach others the truth. This truth comes with great ability to break the bondages of sin and the flesh in your life, and those you minister to!

In addition, every character test you are required to take is not so you will either be rewarded or demoted, but so that you are transformed to becoming a Christ-like, life-giving character. You are therefore not only engaging the enemy, but you are engaging and wrestling your carnal nature to the ground and so being conformed to the process of Christ within you. As Paul said, Christ within, the hope of glory! If you have failed some tests, you just get to write them again until you pass! His grace is enough for you!

BATTLING VOICES-MINDSETS

Mediocre thinking results in poverty mentality and an orphan-like mindset. It has devastating consequences, but only if we allow it or remain ignorant to its influence. Should this stronghold be left unchecked, it will have a much broader and longer effect than most realize. It develops slowly and subtly through unsurrendered lives to the Lord Jesus, and yet He holds the most excellent way of releasing us from this and restoring us.

The most common way to identify an orphan or poverty mentality is thorough character weaknesses developed by past voices and influences of family, culture, or religious and lying spirits.

Your family's mindset will either lead you to poverty or to greatness. For instance, in a family where leaders are spiritually ignorant, they do not see or want to recognize the Lord in their spouses and children. This can also happen in any other environment, like the workplace or school.

Sinful lives cause blindness to God-given potential and getting hung-up by people's humanity, instead of continuing to give what you have received by grace and faith. Such people usually know very little about the creative force of a prophetic word, and do not understand the devastation of words like, *"You will never amount to anything!"*

In some cases, this mentality has become a culture, which becomes very deeply imbedded in ways of thinking that can only be uprooted by the processes of the Spirit of God.

When I was young, a spiritual leader lay hands on me by the Spirit and declared that I would be a ruler and a leader. At that very moment I believed I was spared from developing an orphan mentality ~ my will was established right there in agreeing with God's vision and image of me. Even though my own parents did not raise me, from that time forward I developed an established mindset of success that found security in God my Father.

The prophetic voice brought about an inner breakthrough-ability that could push through any resistance. I truly believed since that day I could be anything, do anything and go anywhere. The leader's voice empowered my will as it spoke to my mind to change the way I think about myself.

BATTLING FLASHBACKS

The greatest challenge for most of us is to avoid living in the past and to see the lingering of such as a temptation of the enemy, for he loves to distract us with our past. As the Lord deals with us in the present, it is very important that we habitually refocus our minds to that relationship with Him based upon His promises.

Sometimes we cannot alter or change what we are currently experiencing. Therefore, we need to come into the habit of *commanding* our thought processes to guard against anxiety.

Some people struggle with phobias like social anxiety, and hesitation (or even fear) to cut destructive relationships and move on to beneficial ones. They may even be stuck in grief over lost relationships due to relocation or being transferred in a career. But our constant friendship with the Lord will supersede any destructive need for relationships that should not, or cannot, be regained.

Take note of the process in the following passage, which comes *before* meditation of Christ. There are active steps to be taken with words like: **"stripping off"** (peeling off; getting rid of; breaking off); **"run"** (no lethargy, dawdling, compromising or procrastinating but going forward and looking ahead); **"focusing"** (look intently, intentionally, concentrate upon); and then **"meditate"** (contemplate; ponder; think; consider; deliberate; reflect).

Can you appropriate these words to your present process or circumstance? My prayer is that you make progress and advance in your walk with God.

Hebrews 12:1-3 (Amp)

"Therefore, since we are surrounded by so great a cloud of witnesses [who by faith have testified to the truth of God's absolute

faithfulness], **stripping off every unnecessary weight and the sin which so easily and cleverly entangles us, let us run with endurance and active persistence the race that is set before us,** *[looking away from all that will distract us and]* **focusing our eyes on Jesus, who is the Author and Perfecter of faith** *[the first incentive for our belief and the One who brings our faith to maturity],* **who for the joy** *[of accomplishing the goal]* **set before Him endured the cross, disregarding the shame, and sat down at the right hand of the throne of God** *[revealing His deity, His authority, and the completion of His work].* **Just consider and meditate on Him who endured from sinners such bitter hostility against Himself** *[consider it all in comparison with your trials],* **so that you will not grow weary and lose heart"**

When I look back at my life, I see that God allowed me to be flexible regarding my dependence upon relationships. And although it might have been painful at times, I am grateful for the Father's teaching. The people I treasured when I was in primary school remain dear friends, and are even like family in some ways, but they are not integrated in my life today. In high school I moved onto different friendships, but I didn't really long for my primary school connections even though some of my best friendships in life were formed there.

After going to Cambridge University and onto Bible School, I made new friends again and they became part of my world.

Today, I do not long for or even regret not having these people in my life for it is more about quality than quantity! Only a small amount of the people from my past is now part of my present life. Many people think that certain relational losses will cause the end of their world but I have learned that you have to embrace the key to emotional and mental health, to adapt to changes, and then embrace the present blessings in your life.

Do not stop hoping and believing, for those God-connections are ordained of the Father to be part of your life. Adopting the mind of Christ about these things will enable you to reach the mental, physical, emotional health and wholeness God desires for you.

Such a connection was made of a friend who attended one of our revival meetings in San Francisco who was suffering psychologically. She had been to countless other meetings and conferences but never received healing. But she never stopped believing that God had that one supernatural connection prepared for her in order to get healed.

After one of our recent revival meetings in San Francisco she shared how, by the grace of God, Master Jesus touched, changed and totally healed her!

Take a moment with me to praise God that He has entrusted us with such yoke-breaking anointing to heal lives!

࿇

PART 4
FRUIT OF MIND-RENEWAL

CHAPTER 16
MEDIOCRE TO EXTRAORDINARY

ೞ

FIRST STEPS

Many people have so many dreams, but there can also be as many obstacles that deter the realization of them. The first step to take is to focus on your thoughts and your mind, not on your actions. What thought patterns are you entertaining? Are they of you, of the devil, or are they from God? You need to simply hear from God.

When I started out in ministry as a young boy, I was already quite experienced in preaching and speaking to people about God. I was preaching everywhere except in my own church.

The pastor didn't give me the speaking opportunity I was hoping for. I was treated with suspicion even though he knew very well what I was capable of. I couldn't understand why he was shutting me down. In frustration, I went to God and I asked Him why this was happening. He showed me the secret motives of my heart and what was stopping my advancing in the work of the Lord. He further revealed that He required me to be an imitator of Himself, and not of man, and that He would open future doors. He said, "If you follow my voice, I will make you great. Do not be intimidated by how long people have been in ministry, but be influenced by what I am doing within you."

After this personal ministry from the Lord my perspective changed ~ I started seeing and thinking of myself differently. Even though I was only about sixteen years old, I started perceiving myself with stature ~ as a man of God. I also started introducing myself to people as such. The day before I was dressing as a teenager, but after that encounter with God I started dressing like a man and perceiving myself as such.

My mindset started changing from being dependent on people for ministry, to taking initiative and expecting God to come through for me. I started identifying myself with characters of the Bible like Joshua, Moses, and Joseph, and placing myself in their company.

This metamorphosis brought me such courage, that I wasn't waiting for an event or an opportunity; I was taking every, and any, opportunity the Lord directed me to ~ even preaching in the streets! I was simply following God's voice while going about my daily business. Each time I asked the Holy Spirit where I should go and what I should do, He replied with a very specific inner instruction. Whenever I boldly acted on God's instruction by faith, I was never disappointed and people's hearts were prepared by God to be open to Him. I realized I was on a very exciting, adventurous lifestyle with God.

These experiences built my faith exponentially. As the Lord gave the opportunities to minister to people, I had a desire to invite them to a regular place of meeting, but I didn't want to call it a church. I knew seeking people like to be associated with certain social clubs, so I started inviting young people to my Bible Club. This became a platform for even greater ministry. I believe the Lord planted these ideas in my mind and I simply had to bring them to fruition. I honestly didn't know what I was doing, yet with obedience I couldn't go wrong! The group was growing and thriving.

Today that first church that denied me ministry opportunity has not grown past three hundred people.

I have a good mind to write a check to that pastor to thank him for not granting me that small-minded opportunity, as it was inadequate to catapult me into the greater things God had prepared for me. As I look back today, God has granted me dreams beyond my expectation ~ He's granted me amazing opportunities to be preaching to thousands all over the world, and He has met all my needs according to His riches in glory!

LEADERSHIP

The mind of Christ belongs to all believers, but each person must choose to develop it, just like a plant needs watering for growth. With the mind of Christ, we were created for leadership in its diverse capacities.

The Word of God has especially granted us this capacity, since Jesus declared of Himself, and of us, that we are light of the world. It seems that the world is getting spiritually darker each passing year but the righteous are getting brighter. This is not only spiritually, but in mind capacity as well. Having Christ in our hearts and minds brings illumination and revelation of the light to the world ~ the answer is in us for each problem.

There is, however, an expectation that even though Christians aspire to be like Christ, those who do not understand the redemptive process of the Holy Spirit in a believer's life will condemn them for not being "perfect"!

This is just where most Christians get "stuck" in sharing their faith with others. But if we share our faith without sharing our testimonies of redemption, which includes the grace of the work of the cross, there will be an emphasis on judging us according to an unrealistic standard of self-righteousness instead of the righteousness of God achieved through the cross of Christ Jesus. Be determined to continue sharing the grace you have received when it seems convenient or not ~ especially those of the household of faith.

2 Timothy 4:2 (Amp)

"...preach the word [as an official messenger]; be ready when the time is right and even when it is not [keep your sense of urgency, whether the opportunity seems favorable or unfavorable, whether convenient or inconvenient, whether welcome or unwelcome]; correct [those who err in doctrine or behavior], warn [those who sin], exhort and encourage [those who are growing toward spiritual maturity], with inexhaustible patience and [faithful] teaching"

CAPACITY TO RULE

The reason why people do not want or trust Christian politicians is because they are thought of not having the capacity for it. This proves that there is still a long way to go in revealing more of the authenticity of Christ in us in certain public arenas.

261

This is not only so people can be professing they know Christ, but primarily are demonstrating His love and power. A true Christian is someone who lives through the indwelling Spirit of Jesus and therefore holds the potential and capacity for all things bringing restoration and life! People who are not introduced to an encounter with the Lord Jesus, either by your testimony or demonstration of His love, will not put their trust in Christian leadership. Not even Christians themselves believe Christian rulers will make it, because of what has been neglected to be preached and portrayed in the past and what is supposed to be demonstrated in speech and deed.

Romans 14:10-13 (Message)

"But you, why do you criticize your brother? Or you again, why do you look down on your [believing] brother or regard him with contempt? For we will all stand before the judgment seat of God [who alone is judge]. For it is written [in Scripture], "As I live, says the Lord, every knee shall bow to me, and every tongue shall give praise to God." So then, each of us will give an account of himself to God. Then let us not criticize one another anymore, but rather determine this—not to put an obstacle or a stumbling block or a source of temptation in another believer's way"

It is time to change our thinking since we have been gifted with the supernatural mind of

Christ. It enables us to accomplish much more than has ever been seen or heard of in our lifetime.

The problem is that we people do not *understand* the Bible. You will find that the children of Israel had the Lord Himself as their ruler and the kingdom was in perfect order. Thereafter, Israel wanted a king but they were incapable to choose a leader unless God did it Himself, as was the case with David and his son, Solomon.

Now the Holy Spirit has been poured out to all who will receive Him so we are already the chosen generation, the royal priesthood as is revealed in Scripture. We lead where He has placed us.

GREATER THINGS

As Jesus commissioned you to walk and do as He did, you have permission to be doing even the greater things that were not documented in the Bible. It's time to know that you have a great advantage as a born-again believer in all spheres of the workplace or in social circles.

My prayer is you will refuse to carry this knowledge with arrogance or pride but with great humility and thanksgiving for what Jesus paid to empower you.

John 14:12 [Amp]

"I assure you and most solemnly say to you, anyone who believes in Me [as Saviour] will also do the things that I do; and he will do even greater things than these [in extent and outreach], because I am going to the Father"

This power has not been granted for your own glory or acknowledgement, but for His ~ even for the humble, everyday aspects of life. Let us progress further into our practice of obedience to the Spirit, by assuming the responsibility of taking this power into our personal neighborhoods, eventually providing benefit to the whole planet. Whether it's a single person, wife, husband, or parent; to being a professional businessperson, teacher, or a politician ~ God has provided supernatural leadership for the advantage of everyone we encounter. Let us refuse to limit the Holy Spirit's work in us exclusively for ministry in the church or for evangelism, but also for the practical, daily needs of our communities ~ who desperately need to see Christ as a reality.

Think of the possibilities and potential you are personally exposed to on a daily basis. Other than choosing Him first at each day, God has also enabled you to make the best practical decisions each day of your life. May the Lord enlarge our capacity of thinking outside the limitations we have set for ourselves and walk in that great and supernatural plan He has for each of us.

In 2015, a Tibetan Buddhist priest embraced Jesus Christ and became a Christian pastor, after seeing the love of Christ shown by a group of Christian workers who helped out and provided relief goods to the people of the region when a major earthquake struck the area.

The seed of Christian love had grown by just one person experiencing the love of Christ ~ who now takes that encounter to a seemingly unreached place.

Philippians 4:13 (Amp)

"I can do all things [which He has called me to do] through Him who strengthens and empowers me [to fulfill His purpose—I am self-sufficient in Christ's sufficiency; I am ready for anything and equal to anything through Him who infuses me with inner strength and confident peace]"

THE HIGHER WAY

As you accept the fervent love of God, also accept a fresh perspective, a new way of thinking the truth ~ that the blood of Jesus covers you and the power of the Holy Spirit guides you and protects you. The presence of the Lord is like oxygen ~ you don't necessarily see Him but you vitally require Him for life. May we all be part of the pure bride that will meet the Lord as conqueror at His return.

People suffer from anxieties and depression, only because somewhere in their past their minds were made up to follow a certain course of action. Those who achieve the most are those who, in spite of these incidents, challenge their minds to accept what has transpired, and to command the mind towards recovery.

You were created to take charge of your mind and instruct it by his Word, because as a child of God you have the authority through the mind of Christ. What you do not see transpiring in your life is what you have neglected to command and speak by the Holy Spirit. Your thoughts will start lining up according to the heavenly standards of His Word, and will start operating in the results you need. Anything you need will come about, even healing for your body and prosperity for your life. The Lord said, in the following Scripture:

Isaiah 55:8-11 (MSG)

"I don't think the way you think. The way you work isn't the way I work." GOD's Decree.
"For as the sky soars high above earth, so the way I work surpasses the way you work, and the way I think is beyond the way you think. Just as rain and snow descend from the skies and don't go back until they've watered the earth, doing their work of making things grow and blossom, producing seed for farmers and food for the hungry, So will the words that come out of my mouth not come back empty-handed. They'll do the work I sent them to do; they'll complete the assignment I gave them."

Together with this higher way of thinking like God, take up and use His word like a weapon (Ephesians 6:10-20). Keep a constant check on your emotions and develop a positive attitude in everything you do. It is a well-known fact that people who are positive live longer than those who think negatively.

The mind of Christ is activated when your heart is in love with Him. Your sweet meditations of Him will develop a calm mind and heart. Allow the creative love-infused Word of God to penetrate your mind in order for it to become part of your daily vocabulary.

As much as the Word of God takes pre-eminence for your mind to operate optimally, take into consideration the chemicals released from the brain through various external stimulants that also affect you either positively or negatively. It is has been proven if you just commit to quietness in the morning and where there are no stimulants, your brain gets an upgrade to boost the functionality of your body.

The Bible is full of guidelines on how to look after your spirit, but also how to keep your body healthy. All lifestyle changes start in the mind. So if there are changes needed to bring health to your body, not only good advice will help do it, but also the application of the mind of Christ for pure wisdom for life. Posture your life to be agreeing with the mind of God and His Word, so your brain is serving you according to God's design. As much as you educate yourself to be aware of the control chemicals have in food or toxins have in the environment, also be aware of those things that hinder emotional maturity and spiritual advancement.

Ephesians 6:13-20 (The Message)

"Be prepared. You're up against far more than you can handle on your own. Take all the help you can get, every weapon God has issued, so that when it's all over but the shouting you'll still be on your feet. Truth, righteousness, peace, faith, and salvation are more than words. Learn how to apply them. You'll need them throughout your life. God's Word is an indispensable weapon. In the same way, prayer is essential in this ongoing warfare. Pray hard and long. Pray for your brothers and sisters. Keep your eyes open. Keep each other's spirits up so that no one falls behind or drops out.

And don't forget to pray for me. Pray that I'll know what to say and have the courage to say it at the right time, telling the mystery to one and all, the Message that I, jailbird preacher that I am, am responsible for getting out"

গুরু

CHAPTER 17
PROPHETIC THINKING

ೞ⊗ೕ

CREATING WITH WORDS

Thinking creatively is thinking prophetically, which is thinking like God. Make sure that you share your God-dreams with the right associates, as this builds faith to fulfill God's dream for you. Be prayerfully selective of friends and family who will support and encourage the realization of the dreams God has spoken over your life.

Joseph received persecution for sharing his dream at an inappropriate time and manner. He almost lost his life, but God's will prevailed as Joseph kept on cooperating with God.

Make sure that your thought processes continually line up what God has already spoken, what you have sensed in your heart, and what you have already confessed with your mouth.

You don't have to be a great orator to engage in this practice ~ you only have to truly *believe* in God's Word for your life, meditating on it daily, and putting the realization of His dream for your life into practice.

It is said that the trouble with talking about your dreams too much, is that it reduces the urgency to be putting it into practice. So make sure your vision is linked to God's mind within a realistic time frame. Therefore, walking in the mind of Christ is truly living to be pleasing unto the Lord. What He has placed in you is what He is thinking, and so doing something about His dream is remaining in the realm of His mind and heart. Thinking prophetically is the start of walking in obedience to the Lord. It is one of the most important things you can learn to do as a Christian.

2 Peter 1:19-21 (The Message)

"We couldn't be more sure of what we saw and heard—God's glory, God's voice. The prophetic Word was confirmed to us. You'll do well to keep focusing on it. It's the one light you have in a dark time as you wait for daybreak and the rising of the Morning Star in your hearts. The main thing to keep in mind here is that no prophecy of Scripture is a matter of private opinion. And why? Because it's not something concocted in the human heart. Prophecy resulted when the Holy Spirit prompted men and women to speak God's Word"

The mind of Christ is a prophetic mind of foresight. It is visionary, farsighted, and somewhat unpredictable. A friend once asked her optometrist to explain the diagram on her wall as to how the process of vision happens. She was fascinated to learn about the connection of the eye to the brain. The optometrist summarized it with: "We don't see with our eyes, we see with our brain."

This concept could also be used to understand how the processes of both our thinking and seeing affect our lives. Jesus said that the lamp of the body is the eye (Matthew 6:22) and how our perception alters and affects our bodies ~ even our whole lives. It is so important that we learn to see supernaturally and prophetically ~ to see as God sees with the mind of Christ.

Apostle Paul placed a very high value on the prophetic gift (1 Cor. 14:1). Of all the gifts he mentioned, he encouraged us to desire the gifts of the Spirit, but especially so that we might *prophesy*. This is because so much of God's vision and purpose for our lives is locked up in this supernatural gift of sight and communication.

As was mentioned, personal prophetic words should be kept within your perpetual consciousness, but they should always line up with God and what He has already intuitively spoken to you. If you receive something new or unfamiliar, take to the Lord in prayer and seek out Godly counsel. His love will always bring you back to the foundation of your relationship in Him.

Uncertain prophesies should be placed under the guidance of seasoned prophets who can help you discern the word of the Lord.

Through all the opportunities that God grants you, you should always keep within His general boundary, God's prophetic vision that He has created through making prophetic words your own. If you keep within this allocation, you will find His provision, glory, and abundance in your sphere.

To think prophetically is lining up your thoughts with the thoughts of God. It is also listening to your subconscious intuitive mind to give you insight into the creative, finer details of your calling. This is truly a key to success.

Generally, our minds do not typically operate if we haven't seen or heard something previously. This limits us and frustrates progress. That is why we need to become much more active in our subconscious minds and imaginations. We need to actually switch on our creativity, which is connected to the Creator.

CREATING WITH GOD

God created us in His image and therefore being creative is something that flows naturally for a child of God. For too long the Body of Christ has been accepting mediocre, uncreative thinking.

When you are *in* Christ you are connected with His mind, emotions, and senses to stimulate a realm of thinking beyond the limitations of the natural mind. His mind has a limitless capacity to create. The following Scripture helps us understand how God builds and plants creatively.

Jeremiah 31:28 (NKJV)

"And it shall come to pass, that as I have watched over them to pluck up, to break down, to throw down, to destroy, and to afflict, so I will watch over them to build and to plant, says the Lord"

Be encouraged to make use of this supernatural gift accessible to each believer to build, develop, create, order, and be fruitful, as God intended it.

God's abundant creativity is within you to be that world-changer ~ to fulfill what Jesus has started. You just need to tap into what He's already provided through your vital connection with Him. As you remain united in His thoughts, you will start receiving solutions for the passions of His heart ~ like provisions for the poor, and justice for the unsupported. You will be that sent-one, by His power, to be the answer to so many prayers.

The book of Genesis reveals that mankind was created in the image of God, which means we are like Him, His representation, His likeness, and His reflection.

Sin altered this state of perfection, not just physically but also in our way of thinking. When we become one with Christ, our spirits become born again and our mind starts waking up to the wonders of God and who He has created us to be.

THE LANGUAGE OF CREATION

First of all, our mind starts communicating adequately – we have a need to remain in unbroken fellowship with the Holy Spirit. This means we start, like babies, learning a new language of the heavenly realm. Our mind also starts to really focus on what is important, to start desiring to walk in godly values and ethical attitudes.

1 Peter 2:2

"As newborn babes, desire the pure milk of the word, that you may grow thereby, if indeed you have tasted that the Lord is gracious"

This new way of thinking by the Word is our new language. It is not a religious babble; it is a pure and practical way of living that is truly creative and innovative.

For example, consider the life story of the famous and creative genius Walt Disney, a former-pastor's son. Although Walt could've been limited by growing up to be like his father, the spiritual values he received from his family catapulted him beyond the limitations of his father's expectations.

Most of his family could not understand Walt's passion for animation and creativity and they felt frustrated with his innovative ways of thinking. In fact, this belief in his dream, caused such a focus and resolve, he was willing to forfeit certain closeness with his family.

He could've easily followed the route of *status quo*, yet he had the inner drive to make his vision a success despite many setbacks and challenges. I believe his godly character and his respect of others undergirded that heavenly gift that made him rise above great adversity ~ making him one of the most innovative minds of his time.

There are many such examples of God using innovative, creative godly men and women, but within each of these stories you will find how the enemy came to thwart and divert them from reaching their goals. Your connection with God is therefore vital to how you partner with God creatively.

My prayer is that you will become so encouraged to not deny or underestimate the importance of developing the use of your creative mind and words as your spirit matures in the Lord. As someone who possesses the mind of Christ, you hold the capacity to co-create and co-design with God. That means you will have that vantage point in the workplace and relationships.

It means you will have that favor you need for people to be open to your ideas. You will become that pivotal leader that a group cannot do without as problems, challenges and crises arise.

The mind of Christ will also operate with a discerning heart ~ a heart full of mercy, grace and love. It is my prayer that the activated spirit of your mind will change your whole life. There are many opportunities right now waiting for you as the child of God to step into, bringing invention and innovation to make our planet a better place.

THE SUBCONSCIOUS CREATIVE MIND

As we are attentive to our thoughts, our words will fall into line with God's thoughts. It is obvious that we want to be more aware of conscious thinking, but being aware of how our minds operate in subconscious thinking is important, but somewhat a mystery.

Subconscious thinking merely needs a cultivation of an awareness that it exists for our benefit ~ that it assists us to think creatively. You cannot force the subconscious, but new thoughts can be dropped into our consciousness from our subconscious minds. Some people know how to use the subconscious more than others, simply because they're aware of its benefit. You don't have to be a special person to learn how to use the subconscious mind.

You only need to be open to God ~ who is consistently speaking to you in the realm of spiritual sight through dreams, visions, and intuitions.

Your subconscious mind can co-operate with the Holy Spirit in bringing inventions and solutions to your mind. These typically come as subtle, small images or words that are dropped into your mind, which act like the mustard seed. When these small seeds of faith-filled visions are developed, they will produce a large tree with much fruit. I've experienced how the Lord has dropped small ideas in my mind and by giving it more thought He has helped me develop it into something beyond my imagination.

God can provide you solutions to accomplish important things, even to the saving of lives. My bamboo bike manufacturing company, Zambikes, located in Zambia, has brought solutions to the problem of limited access to critical medical treatment in rural villages. We named this new invention, the "Zambulance" ~ a two-wheeled ambulance trailer that can easily be attached to virtually any bicycle or motorcycle. It enables patients to be transported to a clinic or other medical facility much more quickly and safely. It also features a steel frame and motorcycle wheels for durability in a punishing environment. It also has a cushion, a reclining backrest, and a weatherproof canopy for the comfort and protection of the patient.

When God gives you a single idea, it develops into greater dimensions of innovation.

After following a single thought from God about manufacturing economical bikes in Zambia, I start asking Him for a goal and a plan. Your subconscious mind will help you with the details because the Holy Spirit resides there, and you will find there is just a flow of living ideas waiting to be tapped! These thoughts can be solutions to your income, debt, ministry, business, marriage, and every area of your life.

Every human being has access to this amazing way of thinking, which has even used by most people without him or her even knowing it. But since you have the mind of Christ, all you need to do is to be aware of how God works in your subconscious mind and then submit to His will. It is very important to know that what God has spoken to you is your greatest asset. The Word of God is your foundation and reinforces these truths. You just need to know how to walk in it as a lifestyle.

Be aware that since your mind is connected with your heart, it has a natural tendency to contradict God. Unrenewed thought patterns could interrupt or even corrupt what God has already spoken to you (see Genesis 3:1 and Jeremiah 17:9). But if you can kick-start that subconscious intuition that God has given today, you will start walking in this great advantage of life.

THE MIND OF GOD IN VISIONS & DREAMS

How does God speak to our subconscious minds? He sometimes speaks directly to us by an inner intuition, a dream, or a vision. See more on how God did this in the case of Joseph the son of Jacob, and Joseph the husband of Mary.

By the awesome creativity of the Holy Spirit we can discern whether a dream granted to us is a spiritual dream, or just a means for the brain to process the events of a day or an issue. I believe the mind of Christ has a subconscious ability to warn us, instruct us or bring clarity through the aid of dreams. Scientists of the world have not been able to fathom the mystery of dreams since they cannot unravel the mysteries of the mind of God. We clearly have the advantage!

Sometimes our dreams are unclear since the Lord wants us to search out their meaning. I believe God uses His creative, sometimes playful humor (in the nature of finding a "treasure"), to allow us to find Him in the process. As we also delve into His Word we inevitably find Him. Scriptures are full of symbolism such as, among others: the journeys of the great faith characters of the Old Testament, the structures of the tabernacles, and the end-time visions of John. All these readings are a means to train the believer how to accurately discern the interpretation of dreams ~ which is God directly communicating with His people.

A dream should therefore not be interpreted by logic or intellectual capacity, but by the sensitivity of the Spirit-mind of Christ through the guided knowledge of the word of God.

If you have asked God for direction or clarity, rest assured, He is literally going to speak to you! Since most of us are occupying our minds so much, He patiently waits for us to fall asleep, to rest our bodies and minds in order for Him to infuse us with His mind. At least have enough sense to go to bed early, eat sensibly, and get enough exercise so that your body and brain is positioned for heavenly connection!

Then once you have drawn near to God, know that He will draw near to you! Be expectant and attentive of these dreams, to faithfully steward the information given to you. He will even at times grant you a random, sudden dream that's not even requested! No matter how detailed or simple the dream is, it will always be backed up by Scripture, and sometimes confirm things you already know. Write the dream out and see how the Holy Spirit leads you on a path of interpretation by Scriptures coming to mind, or finding key words by aid of a Bible concordance. It's fun and exciting to be tapped into the creative subconscious mind of God through dreams and visions.

Keep a dream journal, expect God to speak to you, and determine to be obedient and attentive to His personal prophetic word to you.

CLEAR VISION

Now that know you are able to hear and see the word of God for your life, let us consider how Jesus lived prophetically with the Father.

Jesus' mind was illuminated and He was able to see into the Spirit realm. Whatever He saw the Father doing, he did likewise.

John 5:30 (NKJV)

"I can of Myself do nothing. As I hear, I judge; and My judgment is righteous,

281

*because I do not seek My own will but the
will of the Father who sent Me"*

According to medical research, the brain is
the source of sight. In other words, we do not
see with our *eyes*, but with our *brain*! Likewise,
we are enabled to see what the Father is doing
in the heavenlies by the renewed mind of
Christ!

Being one with the Father, seeing what He
sees, as Jesus did, is how the Holy Spirit also
directs us in life. Throughout Scripture we learn
that where there is spiritual unity with God,
ultimate vision, abundance, and peace
manifests in the natural. The opposite of this
abundance is blindness, complacency and
scarcity ~ the devil aims to *"kill, steal and
destroy"*. Jesus came to do the opposite ~ to
give life and *"life more abundantly"* (John
10:10).

The word "abundantly" is *"perissos"* in the
original Greek, meaning superabundance,
excessive, overflowing, surplus, over and above
more than enough, profuse, extraordinary,
above the ordinary, and more than sufficient.
This is what is in the heavenly realms, and this
is where our thinking is to shift as we get to
know Him.

Not only do we have sight or vision, but we
also have *insight* into the ways of God. We have
access to knowledge that is *reachable*. When
John first announced the coming of Jesus, he

declared, *"The kingdom of God is at hand"* (Matt.3:2). The knowledge of the Lord and His ways are readily available to us and are applicable today.

The words of God are your source of life, whether they are from Scripture or from a prophetic word. This concept has been emphasized throughout Old and New Covenants. Jesus used it as His weapon against the temptation.

Matthew 4:4 (NKJV)

"But He answered and said, 'It is written, "Man shall not live by bread alone, but by every word that proceeds from the mouth of God"'"

Our mind processes things we hear and see. So *how* have you been hearing what the Spirit of God is saying to you? As mentioned earlier, the prophetic words of God are something you should consistently *meditate upon*. This forms a clear and practical vision for your life. It is the single most important thing a believer can cultivate in life.

When I started to grasp the generous and lavish nature of God, I started taking His word and His prophetic words very seriously. Within this process of maturity I started understanding His generous intentions for me. As I continued mastering these thoughts, I began seeing the manifestation of that which I believed. Through meditation upon the good intents of the Lord for me, I started producing and attracting the good and even the great. Some of these happened intentionally, but mostly others happened by God's sudden surprises.

As we start thinking prophetically we tap into an agreement with God's will, and His generosity starts manifesting in our lives.

Many people are who they are today because they have (or have not) discovered this and made a resolve to start thinking like God. It is very important that no matter how small or large your dream or plan is, that you actively start thinking towards the Godly prophetic manifestation of those dreams laid out in His Word, and His personal prophetic word is to you.

Your prophetic words have to be translated into visionary format. These words will allow you to build a reality in your mind's eye. The mind of God, who knows *"the end from the beginning"* (Is. 46:9), will reveal the structure of how His purposes and vision for your life will begin, unfold, and conclude.

HOW TO THINK PROPHETICALLY

Personal prophetic words are simply Scripturally-based words custom designed for you personally! Consider how powerfully the Holy Scriptures have strengthened, guided, and protected you in life. These words have led you to understand the multi-faceted character of the Lord. You've not only become "one" with those words, but also "one" with the author of those words.

Since the cross of Christ is central to our faith, allow me to use the cross as a means to guide you into developing prophetic vision.

Now, in the simplest and most honest posture, connect with the Holy Spirit in the most effective way possible. Ask Him to wrap your imagination around the vision the Father has of you first. Like John the Revelator, be the one who humbly yet boldly declares, *"I am the one leaning on the bosom of Jesus, one of His disciples whom Jesus loves!"* (Paraphrased, John 13:23). Believe that God not only loves all people, but that He loves *you* uniquely and individually.

The best way to make it a reality is by bringing that inner vision of the Lord into your physical senses by sight, sound, touch, taste, and even smell. Be prophetically creative, be honest and use what means the most to you. Create this picture of the vision of the Father for you. Write a song about it, light a fragrant candle as you write the vision in your journal, or place it on your bedroom wall.

Have it physically in your scope of sight.

Start forming an image of that dream or vision that is based upon His word. For instance, do not just meditate on what Jesus has done at the cross, but imagine what that one act is doing for you now, personally. Visualize yourself standing at the scene of the crucifixion, how Jesus thought of you and how His blood flowed for you. Imagine what happened at that point in the Spirit realm ~ how it flowed before the Father as a perfect sacrifice to cleanse you from all sin. Then visualize the effect this is having on your spirit, soul, and body. See your spirit person sparkling, totally clean and free. See yourself as a new person, reinstated to the warm and loving arms of Father God, and how He welcomes you as His own son and daughter.

Imagine, like the prodigal son, being given the grace of all the privileges of your inheritance, even though you might not have deserved it because you squandered it. See how God mercifully welcomes you back, with you enjoying the thought of never being apart from Him again. See your mind in total freedom from condemnation and guilt. Imagine your physical reaction to this sense of freedom ~ abandoned over to worship and praise.

Do you see how you can turn the word of God into pictures for yourself? The word of God is not just a fairy tale or a story ~ it is faith prophetically becoming a reality in your heart. See what impact stories of the Bible have had on people through the creation of movies, videos, and animations?

The Holy Spirit is right here to make every word of God real and personal to you. This process of visualization also pertains to meditation of your own prophetic words, which are mostly about the good and wonderful things God has said over your life and are all in His Word.

By doing this you will start forming habitual thinking around the things God thinks about. The Holy Spirit gives you the creativity in making this part of your conscious and subconscious life. You will start seeing as He sees, and therefore start confessing the truth of what He says. You will begin developing a healthy confidence and a mind that brings honor and glory to God.

WARFARE OF THE PROPHETIC WORD

1 Timothy 1:18 (NKJV)

"This charge I commit to you, son Timothy, according to the prophecies previously made concerning you, that by them you may wage the good warfare, having faith and a good conscience, which some having rejected, concerning the faith have suffered shipwreck"

The process of achieving the reality of the prophetic word is generally not easy, as the enemy knows if he can thwart your faith in the word he may have a means to slow you down. Only you, however, can stop the fulfillment of a prophetic word. The Apostle Paul referred to this process as "waging war".

A practical and personal testimony of the process of waging war with prophetic words illustrates how, first of all, in my quest to know God He was leading me to start praying for the nations. As soon as I started obeying that prompting, my spiritual vision opened up to see a world map. The Lord started building my desire and intellect to reach the nations of the world, despite me having neither a passport nor even the means to travel.

Deep inside He placed a "knowing" in my heart that I would be traveling to all the continents in the vision. This "knowing" is the essence of the prophetic word God gave me.

Soon afterwards I happened to be watching a documentary of India, which revealed more about their culture ~ and especially the issue of idol worship. These images in my eyes spoke and confirmed something in my heart that I would go there someday. The process of prayer and education enabled me to make a decision to go on a mission trip to India after completing my training at Bible School. The warfare of the uncertainty of hearing the voice of God was canceled when I went back to that inner knowing.

Those first encounters with God and the vision of the world map wouldn't leave me. After concluding my work in India, I had an inner prompting for Germany. No matter how intense the wrestle was to join others heading for other nations, my prayers lead me to only focus on Germany.

As a result of this prophetic vision, we were able to impact millions of people during the Soccer World Cup in 2006.

All the while God was expanding my prophetic capacity, and after Germany the urge to advance in business came about. My desire to know more about the kingdom of God relating to business increased. I started focusing on it by studying and planning towards it. I was not only thinking about business prosperity, I was planning towards the success of it. As I was focusing on kingdom mindedness, God sent me friends who were of kindred spirit. This taught me an important lesson on how God values people and relationships above the work or the outcome of that purpose. He taught me to spend less time with people who are not in line with my prophetic destiny.

By thinking prophetically for your life you are not walking aimlessly, being tossed to and fro in relationships that only use you. You already have the word from the Lord that is working to be your leader and governor, and you occupy your thoughts and actions within that capacity. You are thus occupying the territory God has allocated to you by waging the war of your prophetic word. Your prophetic word is the means to your "promised land".

Another discipline came about as I engaged my thoughts to back up what God had already said. I developed a desire to be studying experts in my field through books and videos.

Because of this I can testify by grace, that over the last ten years ministry and business opportunities have miraculously come about to generate great finance for the kingdom. These have come about by either being presented to me, or I was given a creative idea by the Lord to gain kingdom wealth. These words have built my faith and have kept my conscience clear to be operating within the will of God.

In 1999, God gave me a vision to minister and work in America. And through the coaching of the Lord by the prophetic word, it has come to pass and has transformed my entire life and ministry. I am so grateful to our loving Father for His guidance, to reach the great vision He places inside each one of us. If the vision doesn't scare you, it is not God!

So when an opportunity arises which is in line with what God has told you, step-by-step you'll be able to enter into that faith-filled prophetic destiny. You will never suffer "shipwreck" as some of the early believers did. Always follow the purpose, line of vision, and word that God gave you in a dream, during prayer, intercession, word-revelation, or times of prophecy. Anything not in that line of thinking should candidly not be acted upon. You only have to wait upon that timing God has placed in your spirit. He is excited for the fulfillment of your purpose in Him. It is time for you to also get excited, to increase your expectation of the Father fulfilling all He said! It will be right on time!

ෲ

Habakkuk 2:2-3 (MSG)

"And then God answered: 'Write this. Write what you see. Write it out in big block letters so that it can be read on the run. This vision-message is a witness pointing to what's coming. It aches for the coming—it can hardly wait! And it doesn't lie. If it seems slow in coming, wait. It's on its way. It will come right on time'"

CHAPTER 18
NEW MINDSET ON PROSPERITY

ᘓᘔ

Proverbs 10:22 (NKJV)

*"The blessing of the Lord makes one rich,
and He adds no sorrow with it"*

When we esteem riches above spiritual wealth, it will ensnare and be a thorn in our flesh. When God blesses us with spiritual wealth leading to financial wealth, we recognize it is from His very hand and as such brings no sorrow (Prov.10:22).

A heart that trusts the Heavenly Father recognizes true value. Value-standards are measured differently spiritually, than carnal standards.

Such was the case with Mary of Bethany (John 12), who anointed Jesus' feet with a very expensive perfume of pure nard. Studies show that this was thick scented oil obtained from the root of a flowering plant grown in the Himalayas of Tibet, in the northern regions of India and Nepal. To afford such substance was a once-in-a-lifetime privilege that would be reserved only for burial purposes.

In anointing Jesus' feet and wiping them with her hair, it showed that Mary valued the culmination of a year's wages. This, however, was inferior compared to her relationship with the Lord. And lavishing such a generous gift was only appropriate and worthy for the One who would give His very life for her. Mary was thinking from the heart.

May we recognize the priceless value of His presence in our lives, far above the value of money and riches. May we aspire to generously spend our time, talents, and treasure at His feet ~ forsaking the deceitfulness of riches and the anxiety of self-efforts. May we not be like the Pharisaic heart of Judas, who questioned the lavish acts of love being offered to the Lord. The value of pursuing the presence of the Good Shepherd far outweighs anything we can hold in our hands.

Jesus said in John 10:10, He came so that we may have life and enjoy the abundance of it. The Amplified translation expands to, "till it overflows".

My prayer is that you will embrace this reality Jesus has bought for you ~ the care of the good Shepherd who fulfills our every need and so opens hearts and hands to a broken world. When you give in this way, your reward will be supplied in a major way according to what you have sown ~ even thirty, sixty, or one hundred-fold (Matt. 13:23).

May we surrender to His teaching to welcome His excess and abundance. When He took the bread and the fish, it multiplied into twelve basket loads full! This is not poverty ~ this is excess! The pattern of heaven is so lavish that when it is downloaded to you, your home, life, and neighborhood, it overflows in abundance. It is never just about your needs, but also the needs of everyone around you. Even the streets of heaven are made of gold! This mentality is suitable to those made in the image of their Maker.

RELIGIOUS THINKING LEADS TO POVERTY

We do not only see prosperity in heaven but the Bible is full of the declarations of how the righteous live: prosperous, healthy, and wealthy.

The religious and deceptive spirit uses false humility to tolerate the spirit of poverty, since there are those who are convinced that being poor is being spiritually wealthy.

Proverbs 15:6 (Amp)

"Great and priceless treasure is in the house of the [consistently] righteous one [who seeks godly instruction and grows in wisdom], but trouble is in the income of the wicked one [who rejects the laws of God]"

Together with this blessing of the Lord, make sure you maintain the right heart attitude. Decide that your greatest treasures are those stored up in heaven (Matt. 6:20). These treasures are your kingdom-based wishes, your desires ~ those on which your life centers. Your trust in the Lord and your release of anxiety is an open floodgate to your financial provision.

Get into the mind of Christ regarding prosperity! Start living in thanksgiving ~ that God desires to prosper you.

But while He wants you to live in joy and gladness, also be circumspect to the devices of Satan ~ who can only deceive, distract, or deter you from God's best for your life. Paul warns that in the latter times there would be deceptive spirits and doctrines of demons, who aim to deceive many away from the true intentions of God (1 Tim. 4). If a poverty mindset is embraced, Satan will attempt to make it look totally acceptable. Even healthy food and the purity of marriage will appear corrupt.

The same goes for wealth and riches. Forbidding something good that God has ordained to be a blessing, is embracing a hypocritical approach. This is a serious misrepresentation of the Lord. But Paul concludes to Timothy:

1 Timothy 4:4-5 (AMP)

"For everything God has created is good, and nothing is to be rejected if it is received with gratitude; for it is sanctified [set apart, dedicated to God] by means of the word of God and prayer."

SWITCHING OFF POVERTY

Greed and selfishness have taken the place of God-fearing people, making a difference in an honest non-addictive manner. Wealth has now become increasingly associated with those who are *not* God-fearing. Being poor, therefore, has become a warped sense of spirituality and a false sense of humility among Christians. Jesus said in order to follow Him, you are to forsake all, take up your cross, and follow Him. For some, taking up your cross would mean letting go of anything that you depend on more than God.

So if you depend on your humble, poor reputation to gain sympathies, you need to let go and repent. It is all about the heart, the motive in following Christ, for He looks past the outward appearance or achievements and sees the heart (1 Sam.16:23).

The reality is, many Christians have an internal dialogue with themselves along the lines that God does not bless God-fearing people, but only those who are godless. Others go so far as to believe that knowing God can hinder walking in His blessings! It is time to seriously address this mediocre thinking!

To repent means to have remorse, to ask forgiveness, and to feel sorrow. But it also means to have your mind changed, to live differently. We need to repent from the tainted mindset Christians have created about prosperity, and really ask that God would shine His true light on this attribute of His character. This light must be made to shine brighter right now. If we're not careful the enemy will have a foothold to make and keep Christians poor, and so cripple the church from finding greater solutions to the earth's increasing fear and poverty.

Remember, God created every good and perfect gift for our benefit (James 1:17). His will is that no human being is to be suffering from hunger, disease or torment. There is necessity for fasting at times to keep our spiritual senses sharp, but God also makes room for times of feasting. Celebration is part of His annual feasts. God therefore has a very specific purpose for prosperity and overflow, as seen in the lives of characters of the Bible.

When God created the earth, everything was made in perfect balance and perfection. There was no disease or infection present.

All food could be eaten without fearing anything growing on, or inside, the skin that could be harmful. Everything God produced was *"very good"*, for our absolute benefit and intense enjoyment. Considering all this, both man and creation had no reason to grow old or to die. We were created to produce after God's eternal abilities. But as soon as the fall of man occurred, all of creation and everything associated with, or in proximity of, man got exposed to the process of decay.

The mind of Christ grants you the powerful opportunity to bring restoration in every sphere of life. God created you "very good". You are never to accept mediocrity, lack, or failure ~ for the Lord has created you to experience the fullness of His spiritual and physical blessings.

Ephesians 1:3; 22-23 (Amp)

"Blessed and worthy of praise be the God and Father of our Lord Jesus Christ, who has blessed us with every spiritual blessing in the heavenly realms in Christ.

And He put all things [in every realm] in subjection under Christ's feet, and appointed Him as [supreme and authoritative] head over all things in the church, which is His body, the fullness of Him who fills and completes all things in all [believers]"

NO MORE PAUPER-THINKING!

Ecclesiastes 10:7 (Amp)

"I have seen slaves riding on horses and princes walking like slaves on the ground"

Being raised in rural Zambia, I take from my childhood a story that might help you understand how God can take one poor and underprivileged person, and transform him into a testimony of His kindness and generosity. God is still restoring me spiritually, physically, and mentally ~ and He is able do the same for you!

Growing up in Africa, everybody was conditioned to depend on the government for everything. I remember people lining up for sugar and food and there never seemed to be enough for everyone. In those days, having plenty was a foreign concept. At one point I was the owner of only one pair of shoes, and that was not because my parents were without good jobs!

Owning livestock was also a curious thing, as these were not kept to build wealth or even cover reasonable living expenses ~ but reserved to maintain cultural fame and respect. Cows were not bred or slaughtered to earn money, but exclusively kept to slaughter only at weddings or funerals in order to earn community respect. Especially among the Tsonga tribes, wealth was not measured in cash, but in livestock. Gaining the admiration of a whole village or city in this way could easily make a man a king or tribal leader.

It however, did not mean that those tribes were living lavishly or even comfortably, according to modern standards.

Likewise, the church today is filled with God's power and glory. We have the wealth of His presence, but we are always depending on someone else instead remaining in personal and active faith in Him. We are comfortable with having just enough ~ while God has provided supernatural abundance at our disposal for the replenishment and healing of spirit, soul, and body.

God has even blessed the church with brilliant minds to supply vision and governance. But just like the Israelites chose to forfeit their personal relationship with God by appointing Moses, many Christians have maintained a comfort zone in being dependent upon man ~ which has withheld them from providing solutions to worldwide economic problems.

Back in Zambia, my father and uncles had thousands of cows, yet food on the table was a scarcity. In the same way, members of the church have access to all the resources of heaven, but they are choosing to remain disconnected to the endless resources of the Holy Spirit. It is no wonder that counseling rooms are overflowing due to the limited spiritual sustenance. Groups are allowed to be lulled to believe it is acceptable to have become entirely dependent upon one home-group leader, priest, or pastor, and attend church once a week.

It's as mindless as expecting to run a marathon or engage in warfare with the sustenance of one meal a week.

Let us not be like the Zambian tribes, who wait to "slaughter cows" to display their wealth at special occasions! Let us take on the mind of Christ, who does not forsake our expectancy to access God's resources on the earth. Let us not dishonor the Lord by waiting to die to enjoy His wealth in heaven. Let us not be that tribe that waits in poverty to slaughter the cow for the wedding, for a great event, or a conference in which to display God's goodness. God has given me such a heart for the church to be in true health and wealth ~ spiritually, physically, and mentally. Christianity should be associated with the biggest, most brilliant thinkers. Christianity should be linked with great wealth, love, and health since we know the true and living God who dwells in us! Let us not be like the tribe, where we keep a lot of cows but refuse to use any of it for the fear of losing our false humility. We have to let go of our poverty comfort zones and embrace progress in all areas of our lives.

This mindset of slavery will always walk in circles, by talking about the favor and goodness of God, and never take a single step forward to receive access and to enjoy it. Believe today that you are blessed by heaven to be a blessing, a well that is so full that the overflow nourishes others. Be the one that thinks like the King!

Romans 6:20-21 (MSG)

"As long as you did what you felt like doing, ignoring God, you didn't have to bother with right thinking or right living, or right anything for that matter. But do you call that a free life? What did you get out of it? Nothing you're proud of now. Where did it get you? A dead end"

We are living in the times of the "suddenlies" of God. We recently heard a testimony from our miracle services of "miracle money" showing up in someone's bank account, the same way money showed in the mouth of fish (Matthew 17:27). Remember that everything He has promised you shall come to pass. There is a supernatural release of provision and protection. Get ready for a shift of the "tsunami of blessings"!

BREAK THE BAD STIGMA

The reason there is an ungodly stigma to prosperity is because some of us have a preconceived idea that wealth belongs only to the world. The wealthiest people should be Christians, not because there is not a desire to succeed, but because there is a lack of heavenly thinking. If each person on earth had a heavenly mentality, there would be no poverty in the world.

God's original intention for people's lives was to be a reflection of the heavenly realm.

If heaven's streets are made of gold, He intended us to be walking in a realm where there is so much wealth under our feet. He intended that through supernatural thinking, His people would walk in authority and the earth would become restored. We have access to the Creator of the universe, who gifts us with talents and faculties of creative thought to change the world and enhance our environment.

It doesn't mean that you have no influence if you are not personally present somewhere. If God has placed a certain person or group of people on your heart that need restoration, you have access to His courts to bring them before the Father ~ with whom nothing is impossible. Too often the enemy has come to steal what belongs to God, when it has been given to us to reclaim our inheritance.

I pray for greatness in your sphere of influence, for protection from pride or a sense of needing to prove yourself. May you be guarded from a sense of being orphaned or abandoned, so that the glory of God is carried to the next generation. I pray that you will allow the Bible to become alive in you, so that selfish and corrupt thoughts of the world's systems are overcome. The Word of God is your powerful source towards thinking and operating supernaturally. You are entirely covered, nurtured, and have the authority in Jesus' name!

 C>80

John 14:18-20 (MSG)

"I will not leave you orphaned. I'm coming back. In just a little while the world will no longer see Me, but you're going to see Me because I am alive and you're about to come alive. At that moment you will know absolutely that I'm in My Father, and you're in Me, and I'm in you"

CHAPTER 19
YOUR GOLD MIND

CR80

As David created those Michtam Psalms (or "golden songs") in difficult times, God also created your mind to profit from times of praise. Your mind in Christ is that priceless resource. It is like a gold mine.

For instance, a musician practicing a certain sound can be likened to the process of the refining of gold. What he wants to produce, or sound like, originates foremost in his imaginative mind. He keeps sifting and honing his craft, experimenting with various techniques, to eventually produce that golden sound he has referenced in his mind. This is the discerning function in his spirit. For while he is playing, he is searching and seeking until he hits that distinctive tone or melody that reaches a harmony in his soul and affects an audience in so many ways.

In the same manner, your greatness is hidden in your spirit's imagination and intuition ~ and in most cases, like a treasure, is waiting to be sought out or pursued. Do not quit too soon when handling a new idea. Keep digging to find that golden nerve God has given you. If God has given you the vision, He will make sure it will come to pass and you'll find fulfillment in your life. Keep following the voice of the Lord, your source of strength, and He will help you form that creative substance. But you have to stand guard at your "mind-mine", any negative thinking that will hinder your progress.

You can become a much happier person by being in control of your thought life. Do not allow yourself to think negatively, or worry what people have said or thought about you. What about meditating on the good things people are saying about you? What about all you have already achieved?

The most important focus is on what God is thinking about you. Your thought life will inevitably determine your happiness ~ for your profit.

RESOURCEFUL THINKING

The church needs finances to fulfill the great commission. But greater than this is the manifestation of the Holy Spirit's work and fruit in your life, for this is the display of God's glory in the earth.

Within this journey of surrender to His work through you, you will find God meeting all your needs *"according to His riches in glory"* (Phil. 4:19) ~ even prospering you so to meet the expanded vision He is achieving in your life.

In winning souls, He will provide you the strategy how to nurture and disciple them for His glory. When God starts something in you, by the indwelling Holy Spirit you have the guarantee, He will complete and perfect it (Phil. 1:6). Seeking His kingdom and His righteousness as a priority in your life allows the unlimited resources of heaven to be poured out to you, as you remain in thanksgiving and hope of His completion (Matthew 6:33).

This anointing is however only an elementary stage of your fruitfulness in Him, and should never be regarded as "having arrived".

GENEROSITY DEVELOPS WEALTH

One of the reasons why the Gospel has not spread to the unreached parts of the world is that Christians have not had the resources or the means in which to do so. Imagine if each Christian had the mindset to acquire the wealth stored up for them to fulfill the Great Commission. They will be enabled to *"go into all the world"* (Mark 16:15), as Jesus commanded, and be profitable servants unto His glory.

Despite the economic challenges in countries of the world like Africa and parts of South Africa, I've witnessed how God's blessing breaks through mindsets of poverty and defiled religion. The greatest day for the world's nations is when people start recognizing the devil's ways and start being obedient to the Lord who wants to profit us.

The definition of prosperity is being a blessing in order to be a blessing to others. If each Christian has the mindset of really helping only one person a day, our communities will be transformed to prosperity. We are unable to effectively take care of orphans and widows without wealth, so Godly, wealthy mindsets must become our greatest asset.

James 1:27 (Amp)

"Pure and unblemished religion [as it is expressed in outward acts] in the sight of our God and Father is this: to visit and look after the fatherless and the widows in their distress, and to keep oneself uncontaminated by the [secular] world"

Romans 10:9-10 reveals the principle of maintaining a mindset of victory in daily living. God is all-powerful, but He chooses to partner with His kings and priests, and requires us to stand in the authority given to us through the blood of Jesus.

This truth is therefore to be grasped with all intensity and fervor – to believe with our heart and confess with our mouth unto salvation.

The shield of faith is thus held up, and not just to be blocking a bad thought. Both faith of the heart and true confession from the heart are required for the full salvation of Christ in your circumstance. The result is, true heart salvations bring about life transformations, as our minds are covered by the helmet of salvation (as Paul described this in Ephesians 6:17).

The breakthrough power needed to destroy a poverty mindset is the uprooting ability of the dynamic of God's word. The first thing you'll notice with someone who is stuck in a poverty mentality, is their inability to be generous in serving and in finance. The Apostle Luke wrote to the first church about the importance of the practice of giving:

Acts 20:34-35 (AMP)

"You know personally that these hands ministered to my own needs [working in manual labor] and to [those of] the people who were with me. In everything I showed you [by example] that by working hard in this way you must help the weak and remember the words of the Lord Jesus, that He Himself said, 'It is more blessed [and brings greater joy] to give than to receive.'"

This Scripture reveals that being blessed is also having a generous giving and serving spirit. Only through an attitude of giving into good ground, can we receive the riches of God.

Being generous through the Holy Spirit is what keeps us dependent upon the Lord, and therefore always wealthy in heart and finance.

I have learned the art of doing this as a lifestyle, and not because I had a privileged upbringing. During my childhood, circumstances caused me to live in many places, among various types of people. I had to accept my life of living without parents, siblings, or family. I had to get used to the idea of constantly living in-between boarding school, various family members, and friends.

Typically, a person growing up in this environment could have understandably developed a negative mindset concerning families or parents. On the other hand, there lies an advantage in these experiences that awaits everyone who will choose like I did. I chose to focus on what my upbringing gifted me with, that "normal" children could not learn.

It taught me to love people, and to appreciate them just as they are. I've also come to appreciate the power of God in a broken world, and that He can get me out of any problem. Through negative or positive experiences, we all come to form mindsets that shape our lives. So it is so important to train and govern our minds towards success in life.

Many Christians are hurt, disappointed, and even mean. They are stuck because of negative and carnal mindsets that have set in.

They carry experiences from the past and spread this attitude towards the body of Christ.

We have to view everything from the light of Christ. *"In His light do we see the light"* (Ps. 36:9). It is time that we break into the light of the mindset of the mind of Christ. And generosity is not always about money or finance. It is also being generous by serving others with our time and talents. There are so many ways we can offer God a seed through faith ~ a seed He can transform into Christ-like, wealthy living. When we embrace the immeasurable generosity of God through Jesus Christ, there is a natural progression of wanting to bless and give to others. Giving is, and continues to be, a necessary means God uses to keep us free from poverty, and abounding in wealth and riches.

The principles of the Word of God are so important to break off this spirit. Jesus used a parable to clearly warn us should we not guard against its corruption. Jesus said that wealth, which replaces the dependence upon God, is like an injurious thorn in our flesh:

A SOUND MIND AND BODY

Matthew 13:22 (Amp)

"...And the one on whom seed was sown among thorns, this is the one who hears the word, but the worries and distractions of the world and the deceitfulness [the superficial pleasures

*and delight] of riches choke the word,
and it yields no fruit"*

You are about to become very wealthy in the Lord, as you are becoming sound in your thoughts and actions. It will bring wholeness and advancement in your body too! It does not depend on your upbringing and circumstances.

The prophetic voice of God over your life is just so much stronger than your present circumstance. Lift your eyes afresh in faith of your Heavenly Father today. Do not lean on the arm of flesh, but lift your hands in surrender to His faithfulness and purpose. You are only to believe His infallible promise to your personally!

A testimony was recorded of a woman who attended our meetings, declaring that an $11,000 debt was supernaturally "forgiven" by the bank! Previous to this miraculous news, she had made plans to sell things so that she could pay the debt. But the Holy Spirit told her to wait and to watch Him move on her behalf.

Previously she had been so anxious about this debt. But despite the stress she had that inner knowing that God was taking care of her. When she received the call from the bank exonerating her from all debt, she thought it was a prank call. After she hung up the phone, she thought to call again to check if it might be true. The bank confirmed the same information again. It was then it dawned on her that God had supernaturally favored her by the whole amount being settled so that she could walk in financial freedom.

There is "gold", and other physical resources available to us if we'll just learn to trust and focus on our endless Provider!

In a meeting in August 2015, I was praying for the finances of people, and a woman testified that some great changes had come into her finances after the meeting. She told that there were certain things from her family and her past that had been "blocking" the blessing of God. She mentioned her late father who was schizophrenic and her mother also suffering greatly because of this. She experienced the battling of so many strongholds while she was growing up in her parents' home. She said that when hands were laid on her at the meeting, she believed the breakthrough of a sound mind was restored to her.

She now testifies of receiving full financial restoration, and that she has become so prosperous. She is now able to fund the Gospel and take care of her children. Instead of her children cursing God because of the poverty suffered, they are now a blessing of the Lord to see the restoration of their own lives.

Revelation 3:18 (MSG)

"Here's what I want you to do: Buy your gold from me, gold that's been through the refiner's fire. Then you'll be rich. Buy

your clothes from me, clothes designed in Heaven. You've gone around half-naked long enough. And buy medicine for your eyes from me so you can see, really see"

Your prophetic word holds the resources of heaven, not only in renewing your mind but also providing the means by which you will fund the Gospel, your ministry, and your life. You hold the ability to be a good, diligent steward and so receive the reward of the Lord.

Hebrews 11:6 (NKJV)

"But without faith it is impossible to please Him, for he who comes to God must believe that He is, and that He is a rewarder of those who diligently seek Him"

❀

CHAPTER 20
A MIND OF PASSION

ೞ

1 Corinthians 14:2, 4 (NKJV)

"...for he who speaks in a tongue does not speak to men but to God, for no one understands him; however, in the Spirit he speaks mysteries.... He who speaks in a tongue edifies himself"

PRAYER & PRAYING IN TONGUES

As you renew, cultivate, and defend your mind in Christ, you will be experiencing the passion of the Lord for your heart and life. Just like Jesus, you are on His journey of living out a passion for the Father. Just like Jesus lived with zeal about the things that mattered to God, so your mind is becoming focused by renewal. Jesus was full human, but was also fully God incarnate. He came to demonstrate what true humanity should be, and relates to us in the fullest degree even though He is perfect and holy.

317

But just like anything in the natural, at times you will feel dry and have a need to be refreshed and encouraged. Before you go and see anybody to pray with you, consider meeting the Lord in your inner closet. You are bringing your mind to a place of refreshing to receive from the Lord.

To have your mind continually converted is a process of ongoing repentance. It is a place of taking up your cross, laying down your life, and finding a place of refreshing as you posture yourself humbly in your walk with God. Repentance however, has a process in order for permanent change to take place. It is receiving the ability to see as God sees ~to truly see the consequence of your actions and how it is affecting God's heart and those who you are hurting.

Acts 3:19 (NKJV)

"Repent therefore and be converted, that your sins may be blotted out, so that times of refreshing may come from the presence of the Lord"

There is also another spiritual element that must not be neglected in the process of being transformed. Most of the time we do not know where to start in our communication with the Lord, but repentance is always a good place. We do not always know what is appropriate, or even how to say what is on our heart. But the Lord knows His own mind as we've learned, and we do not always know how to tap into it.

God, however, knows our thoughts and therefore He has given a way to commune with Him that supersedes language. He has given us a way to activate extraordinary communion beyond praying the Lord's Prayer, or even all the other prayers modeled in the Bible.

Many times our minds are so filled with thoughts of the day, while managing so many things that occupy us, that it is difficult to switch into a spiritual mode. Sometimes you only gain a "momentum" in your communion with the Lord after heartfelt repentance has taken place.

Other than reading Scripture, which often takes time, tongues were given to the body of Christ as a "super-gift" to be used during private worship. Too little emphasis is being placed in leaders teaching this, as it holds tremendous, brilliant benefit yet it is not meant to be "man-ward". The gift of tongues is an instant "God-ward" gift unless the gift of interpretation is used, so hearers may understand. Since man is not the goal it takes on a spiritual expression. The seat of this expression is therefore not the mind, but the Spirit, for God is Spirit (John 4:24).

Therefore, being spiritually strengthened through prayer whether it be through heart-felt prayer with language, or in the Spirit's language, is a mindset that will allows you to remain built up, encouraged, and comforted in your walk with God.

319

This is also thus, a vital part of walking in the mind of Christ. I've often seen and heard how ministering in the Spirit in preaching, teaching, and praying for healing is accompanied with the spontaneous eruptions of speaking in tongues. Even in driving out demons from people, the Holy Spirit has led us to be praying in tongues, to which He grants us strength, authority, and interpretation of the situation.

A MIND OF PRAISE

Praying with the mind of Christ is therefore praying in both our mother tongue, but also in the language of the Holy Spirit. In both manner of praying, they come from the Spirit instead of the intellect, and the same is true for singing praises. For Apostle Paul, praying and singing with the aid of tongues was a lifestyle. He was being naturally supernatural.

Each time I would be praying or singing in tongues, I would come to a refreshed view of the name of Jesus and also my position in Christ. I would receive a rest and a refreshing that cannot be attained in any other way. I've noticed that within this mode of refreshing I am able to comprehend the Word of God in the mind of Christ. I am not refreshing myself with sensual indulgences, but I am delighting myself in the Lord!

Ephesians 5:17-19 (NKJV)

"Therefore do not be unwise, but understand what the will of the Lord is. And do not be drunk with wine, in which is dissipation; but be filled with the Spirit, speaking to one another in psalms and hymns and spiritual songs, singing and making melody in your heart to the Lord..."

As prayer is a spiritual engagement that cannot always be understood by the natural mind, the mind of Christ is actively involved in the use of praying in tongues.

Romans 8:27

"Now He who searches the hearts knows what the mind of the Spirit is, because He makes intercession for the saints according to the will of God"

The mind of Christ knows the will of God, and so praying with the aid of the Holy Spirit is vital for your spiritual growth. It is therefore not a good idea to always be praying silently, for the Lord has deeper revelations into His love for your life that you will pick up during this time of prayer with Him. Find a "private closet" where you can be shut in from distractions, where you can be uninhibited to really connect with God. Jesus advises how to go about this in Matthew 6:5-14.

The language of the Spirit is a gift of grace, so therefore you need to alter your thinking from engaging your intellectual thinking to synergizing your heart, will, and intellect to the Lord.

When speaking in tongues, you become like a life-giving "babbling brook", a wellspring of life operating in the flow of the Holy Spirit. It is a spontaneous flow, a release of inner emotions and words that could not be uttered. You are strengthened and enabled; you become watchful and persevering by praying in this way.

Ephesians 6:18 (NKJV)

"Praying always with all prayer and supplication in the Spirit, being watchful to this end with all perseverance and supplication for all the saints"

Pray with me in the name of Jesus that if you have not received the gift of Holy Spirit tongues, you be baptized with this ability in order to operate in the fullness God has in store for you. The original outpouring of the Holy Spirit in Acts 2 was marked with this manifestation of the Spirit, only the recipients could also speak in known languages that could be understood by foreign nationalities for the sake of spreading the Gospel. The Lord has this amazing gift in store for you. You only need to ask for it.

Many have received this gift by simply spending time with others who pray in this manner. It is sometimes an activation that can be imparted to those who spend time in the anointing of another believer.

You will find how praying in this manner reactivates you spiritually. You will find that the many spiritual gifts will be loosened to be applied for a given task or a situation. I believe that each child of God was meant to operate in all the spiritual gifts of 1 Corinthians 12, and therefore, as we pray in the Spirit, we will be more open to operate in them at every opportunity.

Speaking in tongues does not necessarily have to be a mindless activity, for you can also pray that the Lord give you interpretation of your own tongue or the tongue of another believer.

In 1 Corinthians 12, Paul introduces guiding principles that distinguish the ways of the Holy Spirit. The power of the Holy Spirit does not drive people into wild, mindless, compulsive acts. His gentle ministry strengthens human personality. He does not overpower. All manifestations of the Spirit also glorify Jesus and will harmonize with the truth about Him. The main work of the Holy Spirit is to bring people under the lordship of Jesus.

Jesus prayed from a position of "Sonship". We see this in the account of Jesus resurrecting Lazarus. May we, like Jesus, have this mind of covenant, the thoughts of the Lord in our prayers.

John 11:41-42 (NKJV)

"Then they took away the stone from the place where the dead man was lying. And Jesus lifted up His eyes and said, "Father, I thank You that You have heard Me. And I know that You always hear Me..."

BUILDING YOURSELF UP

Jude 20

"But you, beloved, building yourselves up on your most holy faith, praying in the Holy Spirit"

Thoughts focused on self and on the things of the world will break you down little by little. Therefore you should always have a mindset of building yourself up to counteract and contradict these thoughts. You were meant to have the mind of Christ and live above these attempts of oppression.

As the great High Priest, Jesus is always praying for us. And since we remain in covenant with Him, we are simply falling in with the prayers He is already praying in heaven. The Holy Spirit has made this possible by supplying us an accent or a rhythm of heaven, which is the language of the Spirit.

Hebrews 7:25 (NKJV)

"Therefore He is also able to save to the uttermost those who come to God through Him, since He always lives to make intercession for them"

A vital part of your spiritual growth is praying in one's own language as prompted by the Spirit. Romans 8:15 and 26 speaks of the Spirit praying with *"groanings which cannot be uttered",* and praying in a tongue unknown to the one praying, yet the Spirit is praying through you without your natural mind understanding.

Once I felt stuck in a challenge. I didn't know what to do and didn't know the solution to a problem. Then as I prayed in the language of the Holy Spirit, I started getting an "interpretation of tongues" and I knew exactly what I needed to do. I saw the way, and the new idea just popped up!

Other times, crossroads were before me, or someone would ask me for wisdom and counsel. Naturally, I didn't have the immediate solution and I didn't know what to do or what to say, since working with people is generally sensitive in nature. As I prayed in and with the Holy Spirit, I automatically had answers. My spiritual insight opened up and wisdom flowed from my mouth. Literally, the Holy Spirit enlightened my mind and it seemed I was such an astounding person. But I knew without a doubt I was flowing and glowing in the amazing grace of His mind.

Many times ministry opportunities are presented to me, but an open door or a friendly reference is not necessarily of the Lord or in His timing. So praying in the Spirit before I make any decision has become vital in my lifestyle walk with God. My natural mind is not my leader, but it is a *servant* of the mind of the Lord, and so prayer in this manner activates my mind and makes my brain operate optimally.

Living by faith and within total dependence upon the Lord in life and ministry entitles you and me to boldly ask the Lord for provisions. This is simply His will as He cares for us.

Prayer however, does not provide wealth or provision, but it provides me the connection with heaven to "download" wisdom and illumination. It provides us the *what, when, and how* to go about operating in kingdom procedures.

Like the menorah lampstand in the Holy Place, prayer provides the light to see the open door that was once was obscure. It not only provides us the silhouette of something, but the noonday sun's light on a situation. What was previously obscure then becomes abundantly clear. So much so, that you are enabled to even tap into the emotions and heart of God. The right decisions, words, and path of life will be revealed to you. His heart gives you the interpretations of the emotions of the Lord. You feel what God feels, and so you are enabled to make the right decisions. You are ignited in God and so it brings you into His glory realm. This is the mind of passion that He desires for each one of us.

My prayer today is that the Lord will grant you this passionate vision of heaven with Jesus interceding for you at the right hand of God. He is able to save you to the uttermost, He is able to complete what He has started in you, and there is therefore nothing He cannot handle on your behalf.

THE NECESSITY OF CORPORATE PRAYER

People of life-giving success are people who know how to pray.

Other than praying in the Holy Spirit, it is always good to refer to the model prayers of Jesus, the prophets, and the apostles for inspiration. We see the powerful results of unified prayer in the early church and how these powerful prayers opened prison doors and even saved the lives of believers.

In our time effective spiritual leaders who have walked the path of longevity in the Spirit, are those who have an active stamina and a ministry priority in the realm of prayer. Part of thinking like Christ is to be able to pray, petition, and to intercede like Him. But in essence, the mind of Christ is shared with us so we will be identified as one with Him. As important as personal and daily prayer is, intentional, regular public prayer unites our hearts and minds in Christ. It provides us that endurance and tenacity needed in laying our lives down for the cause of Christ. If ever we needed Christ in the nations of the world, prayer is that catalyst that will keep us arising and shining in a broken and lost world. May you be the instigator of prayer wherever you go, as your vital need and necessity in every situation.

I was so delighted, privileged, and blessed to be uniting in prayer at the Azusa prayer event in Los Angeles this year. This life-changing occasion brought the church together like never before, and it is the one event that stands like a beacon in thousands of lives.

Away, was the need for schedules, entertainment and information. In, was the desperate need to just glorify the Lord, connect with Him, and hear the "now-word" from heaven for our nation. Heaven replied passionately with many testimonies of miraculous signs, healings, wonders, and prophetic words to nations, groups, and individuals ~ as the Lord swept us away in His glorious zeal. I believe this was a pivotal point in our nation and in the world.

Jesus prayed in John 17:22:

"And the glory which You gave Me I have given them, that they may be one just as We are one. I in them, and You in Me, that they may be made perfect in one, and that the world may know that You have sent

Me, and have loved them as You have loved Me"

FASTING

When Jesus was transfigured on the Mount (Matthew 17), his inner group shared the spectacular experience with Him. I am sure they came off the mountain in total spiritual euphoria, because Peter even offered that they "camp out" on that mountain with Elijah and Moses.

On their way back down, however, they were met with a desperate obstacle ~ the reality of the day with the disciples needing to exorcise a suicidal demon of epilepsy that just wouldn't budge!

Jesus took charge of the situation and cast it out of the child, but later spoke to the disciples about something they overlooked.

Jesus said *"this kind does not go out except by prayer and fasting"* (Matthew 17:21), but He also coupled this teaching with the issue of unbelief. He said that it is not how big or small your faith is, because even a *small* amount of faith *applied* can move the greatest obstacles.

Matthew 17:20 (NKJV)

"Because of your unbelief; for assuredly, I say to you, if you have faith as a mustard seed, you will say to this mountain, 'Move

329

*from here to there,' and it will move; and
nothing will be impossible for you"*

I believe there is little power in fasting itself. The real power lies in a greater concentration of connection with the Lord, and having your mind not set on your survival but on *dependence* upon God. As we are building our hearts and minds in the Lord, we are building our *capacity* of faith in Him. Faith therefore, must be nurtured and grown to maturity. Sometimes our spirits are praying, but we need the servanthood of our bodies to be praying as well. Our emotions, monthly cycles, and circumstances can sometimes withhold us from spiritual growth. That is where Spirit-led fasting takes a hold of these distracting issues.

Although both fasting and prayer can also become a ritual, through the Holy Spirit's aid, physical practices are ways the Spirit can use to align our faith to be spiritually powerful in the earth. Faith that appears small or weak to us, still can accomplish the humanly impossible.

Engaging in fasting speaks of believers who through commitment, accurately understand their authority and know God's power, His will, purposes, and provision.

A HEART OF CONVICTION

A heart only becomes a passionate heartbeat by conviction. The Holy Spirit is the one who convicts and convinces us of God's mind. Only then are we producing true spiritual fruit and become productive in life. Paul had to become fully convinced and persuaded of God's love before greater manifestations of the Spirit and miracles started happening (Romans 8:38-39).

Are you maintaining in your faith shield? Are you fully persuaded and convicted that He has chosen and bought you with a price? Are you convinced that you belong to the Lord, that He has granted you success, wealth, and victory ~ and that He is *for* and *with* you?

One can see the evidence of a life not fully persuaded, when they are merely echoing the voices of others revelations in their pursuit of God.

But when they become an intimate, prayerful, authentic voice, producing fresh revelation from the presence of God, the full conviction and persuasion of the salvation process has started taking place and their confession holds power. This is the Word that the Lord confirms with signs and wonders following, as His revelatory Word delivered is the presence of Jesus Himself.

In Acts 14, Paul and Barnabas had to remain many days in Iconium and persisted amidst persecution and resistance of the Gospel. But because they endured, signs and wonders starting happening and granted them heavenly confirmation of their conviction. You cannot be persuaded if you are not willing to endure the resistance with a convicted heart of prayer. Prayer enables you to be convicted by His mind rooted in your heart. Paul was convinced he had become one with the mind of Christ, which became the revelation of the New Testament. His faith in the Words of Jesus was so persuasive that he was even willing to lay down his life for it.

I pray this Scripture locates you as to where you are in your journey of becoming persuaded and thus passionate, towards the Lord's mind for you! With God, all things are possible!

2 Timothy 1:12 (Amp)

"This is why I suffer as I do. Still, I am not ashamed; for I know Him [and I am personally acquainted with Him] whom I have believed [with absolute trust and confidence in Him and in the truth of His deity], and I am persuaded [beyond any doubt] that He is able to guard that which I have entrusted to Him until that day [when I stand before Him]"

IN CONCLUSION

MY PRAYER FOR YOU

*I pray in the Name of Jesus that every person that will read this book will have their mind **renewed** to acquire a perspective of their God-given mind. They will look at their mind as a gift and not an enemy.*

*Father, I pray that the mind of Christ, which is being in Christ, will transpire in a people who think, speak, and operate in the **ways of Christ**. Let kindness, love, respect, and perseverance become part of their thinking. Let them prefer one another and think of others more highly than themselves.*

*I pray for that renewed mind of Christ, knowing that He came and suffered so that we can **excel, exceed, and shine**. He came so we could be the light and dispel the darkness.*

*Lord, I pray You will protect our mind from things that are not of the light so that our hearts will **remain pure**. Keep our minds from accepting things that do not line up with Your Word.*

*I pray You will increase the **capacity** of our minds concerning the things of God, but also create a capacity in our hearts to cooperate with You. May each person be an obedient child that will accept the Word of God, so that knowledge* *in our heads will become an eternal treasure in our hearts.*

*I pray that this knowledge of You will not become defiled through suffering, rejection, or pain of the world. **Protect** this happiness You cause to be stored in our hearts. Let us keep our hearts married and faithful to You by feeding our minds with the Word of God, and listening to positive things. Lord, cover our minds with the **blood of Jesus** and I pray, Spirit of the Lord, may we have Your supernatural and extraordinary mind to enable us to co-create with You ~ a mind that will bring reality to the dreams You have placed in our hearts and minds. I pray this in Jesus' name. Amen.*

May His passion consume you to draw closer to Him ~ and so become all He has designed you to be.

☙❧